WITHDRAWAL

NEW DIRECTIONS FOR ADULT AND CONTINUING EDUCATION

Susan Imel, *Ohio State University*
EDITOR-IN-CHIEF

An Update on Adult Development Theory: New Ways of Thinking About the Life Course

M. Carolyn Clark
Texas A&M University

Rosemary S. Caffarella
University of Northern Colorado

EDITORS

Number 84, Winter 1999

JOSSEY-BASS PUBLISHERS
San Francisco

AN UPDATE ON ADULT DEVELOPMENT THEORY: NEW WAYS OF THINKING
ABOUT THE LIFE COURSE
M. Carolyn Clark, Rosemary S. Caffarella (eds.)
New Directions for Adult and Continuing Education, no. 84
Susan Imel, Editor-in-Chief

Microfilm copies of issues and articles are available in 16mm and 35mm,
as well as microfiche in 105mm, through University Microfilms Inc., 300
North Zeeb Road, Ann Arbor, Michigan 48106-1346.

ISSN 1052-2891   ISBN 0-7879-1171-2

NEW DIRECTIONS FOR ADULT AND CONTINUING EDUCATION is part of The
Jossey-Bass Higher and Adult Education Series and is published quarterly
by Wiley Subscription Services, Inc., a Wiley company, at Jossey-Bass, 989
Market Street, San Francisco, California 94103-1741. Periodicals postage
paid at San Francisco, California, and at additional mailing offices. Postmaster: Send address changes to New Directions for Adult and Continuing Education, Jossey-Bass, a Wiley company, 989 Market Street, San
Francisco, California 94103-1741.

SUBSCRIPTIONS cost $65.00 for individuals and $135.00 for institutions,
agencies, and libraries.

EDITORIAL CORRESPONDENCE should be sent to the Editor-in-Chief,
Susan Imel, ERIC/ACVE, 1900 Kenny Road, Columbus, Ohio
43210-1090. E-mail: imel.1@osu.edu.

Cover photograph by Wernher Krutein/PHOTOVAULT © 1990.

Jossey-Bass Web address: http://www.josseybass.com

Printed in the United States of America on acid-free recycled paper con-
taining 100 percent recovered waste paper, of which at least 20 percent is
postconsumer waste.

CONTENTS

EDITORS' NOTES

It is hard to imagine the field of adult education apart from the literature on adult development; many aspects of our thinking about adult learners and the learning process are shaped by our knowledge of how adults change and develop across the life span. It is essential, then, for us to stay current with the advances in this rich and influential literature. The purpose of this volume is to help us do that.

An *Update on Adult Development Theory* captures some of the most recent work across the broad domain of adult developmental literature and assesses its significance for us as adult educators. Our first task in designing the volume was to figure out how to make sense of this diverse and multidimensional literature. We wanted to revisit the more traditional theories and see what new ideas were being generated there, but even more we were interested in seeing in what new ways the life course was being theorized.

The four-part typology of Merriam and Caffarella (1999), consisting of biological, psychological, sociocultural, and integrative models of development, seemed to serve us best, and it provided the underlying structure for the volume. We identified major topics in each of those areas that addressed different dimensions of development and invited chapter authors to explore them. We asked that they review the major tenets and assumptions of their topics, discuss the most salient work, and assess the implications of this work for adult learning.

We begin the volume with our chapter on the whole project of theorizing about adult development—determining its definitional boundaries and deciding its scope—and discuss how those decisions are made by theorists. Then we explain the typology of developmental theories that serves as the framework for the volume.

In the first section, consisting of two chapters, we look at the more traditional perspectives on development—the biological and psychological aspects. Vivian W. Mott explores the complexities of biological development and aging, as well as work on the mind-body connection. Then Patricia M. Reeves summarizes the major research done from the psychological perspective, both the classical theories and the newer work that has arisen from their critique.

The next section addresses the social and cultural aspects of our lives that drive growth and change in adulthood. In her chapter, Jovita M. Ross-Gordon explores the complexities of gender development and what it means to develop as a woman or a man in our culture. Next Alicia Fedelina Chávez and Florence Guido-DiBrito examine how we develop our sense of ourselves as members of a racial or ethnic group. Then Kathleen Edwards and Ann K. Brooks look at sexual identity development, focusing primarily on sexual orientation as a core aspect of this developmental process.

We next investigate some of the integrative models of adult development—models that incorporate multiple dimensions of development. The chapters in this section suggest some of the rich possibilities of this approach. Kathleen Taylor, in her chapter, examines the tension between separation and connection in developmental theory, focusing on several theories that seek to strike a balance between these two powerful drives. Then Sharan B. Merriam explores the biological, sociocultural, and historical understandings of time and applies these notions to the experience of HIV-positive adults. Next Marsha Rossiter looks at the storied nature of development and provides an entirely different perspective—one that views development as narrative and places the adults themselves in the role of interpreter. Finally, Elizabeth J. Tisdell discusses the notion of spiritual development and explores the various cultural manifestations of this significant aspect of adult growth.

We close the volume with a final chapter in which we assess the state of adult developmental theory overall, focusing especially on the integrative mode that currently dominates the literature. From this material we draw some implications for the field of adult education.

M. Carolyn Clark
Rosemary S. Caffarella
Editors

Reference

Merriam, S. B., and Caffarella, R. S. *Learning in Adulthood: A Comprehensive Guide.* San Francisco: Jossey-Bass, 1999.

M. CAROLYN CLARK *is associate professor of adult education at Texas A&M University, College Station.*

ROSEMARY S. CAFFARELLA *is professor of educational leadership at the University of Northern Colorado, Greeley.*

1

This chapter outlines a typology of developmental theories that consists of biological, psychological, sociocultural, and integrative models.

Theorizing Adult Development

M. Carolyn Clark, Rosemary S. Caffarella

The whole point of theory—any theory—is to help us understand something better. This volume examines the theories that have been constructed about adult development, and the "something" that all these theories are trying to help us understand better is the life course—how it unfolds and the meaning that can be given to various aspects and dimensions of that unfolding. A particular theory or family of theories serves as a kind of lens through which we view the life course; that lens illuminates certain elements and tells a particular story about adult life. Multiple lenses give us many different ways of illuminating different aspects of that life course. The purpose of this volume is to provide an overview of those lenses.

This chapter presents the frame for the volume. First we address central issues inherent in any discussion of adult development—issues that define the parameters of the concept of development and shape the production of theory. Then we examine a four-fold framework for categorizing adult developmental theories.

Defining Adult Development

One of the striking things about adult development as a field is its age. It is entirely a twentieth-century phenomenon, in no small part because the concept of adulthood has crystallized only in this century. Jordan (1978) tracks the evolution of the concept in America and argues that rapid social change is responsible for a shift from condition to process: "In our culture, adulthood as a condition used to be simply assumed; as a process, it now seems to demand explanation" (p. 198). It is precisely understanding this process that is the focus of developmental theory.

There are many vexing definitional issues here. For starters, when does someone enter adulthood? Answers are highly domain-specific. Legally, in the United States at least, this varies by state and by specific arena. There are stipulated ages at which a person may work, drive, vote, marry, or join the armed forces; these ages differ from state to state. But legal definitions set only one type of boundary. Culturally, in this country, people are considered adults when they are responsible for themselves and often for others, but these boundaries are also blurred. A college student, for example, can be living on her own but be fully supported financially by her parents. Or a fourteen-year-old can be living with his family and working after school to help support the household. A common convention among theorists is to use age eighteen as a benchmark, because this marks the end of mandatory schooling and is the typical point at which young people begin to assume responsibility for themselves and others (Bee, 1996). But this is an approximation at best.

More complex is defining the process of adult development itself. What exactly do we mean by development? Of course development involves change over time, but that isn't sufficient. Meacham (1997) argues that development involves change that is orderly and predictable, producing results that are "both irreversible and novel" (p. 43). So there is a certain sustainability and newness here. Bee (1996), following Werner and Kaplan (1956), defines development as "increasingly higher, more integrated levels of functioning" (p. 15). This adds the notion of greater complexity to the mix, as there is an implicit sense that a normative standard shapes the developmental trajectory, in this case the valuing of sustainability and complexity. In more recent years this normative standard of development has been as aspect of critique in the field (see, for example, Tennant and Pogson, 1995).

Then there are the tensions around what, exactly, is caught in the net of developmental theory. We study individuals so that we can generalize beyond them, but how can we account for both individual uniqueness and commonalities across groups? And how can continuity and change be explained, both in terms of the sense of self that endures and changes across the years and the life course itself, during which we experience periods of stability and periods of major change? And the thorny issue of differences (gender, race and ethnicity, class, education, sexual orientation, personality, intelligence, to name some of the big ones) arise, along with the question of how those differences affect development. How does all this get captured in adult developmental theory? Imperfectly, it seems. No one theory explains everything, but each provides a particular way of looking at adult development and illuminating certain aspects of it. The richest insights into the life course come from the application of more than one theory (see, for example, Daloz, 1986).

A Typology of Developmental Theories

So many theories are out there that it is helpful to make sense of the whole first—to categorize them by purpose or orienting assumptions—so that we can see what each cluster is seeking to accomplish. There are many ways to do this, but we are most persuaded by the typology offered by Merriam and Caffarella (1999). Building on the work of Perlmutter and Hall (1985), Bee (1996), and others, they have developed a schema consisting of four components: biological, psychological, sociocultural, and integrative models. Although they recognize that not all theories fit neatly into one of these categories, this framework does provide a useful starting point for understanding the many-faceted ways of thinking about development in adulthood.

Biological Perspective. The biological frame acknowledges that we are physical beings; as such we will change physiologically, whether those changes are driven by natural aging, the environment, our own health habits, or by an accident or disease process. Our ideas about biological aging tend to be negative and associated largely with decline. The stereotypes we hold about the physical aging process are strong and prevalent within our own psyches and are embedded in societal expectations and norms. The fact remains that, although the life expectancy of adults in the Western world has doubled over this past century, "our capacity to live longer does not mean we have been able to halt the primary process of aging—those time related physical changes governed by some kind of maturation process, as in vision and hearing, for example that happen to all of us" (Merriam and Caffarella, 1999, p. 95). Still, current literature stresses that the natural physical changes that we all will experience won't affect us much until our sixth and seventh decade. Even then researchers are questioning whether some of the assumptions we have been making about biological aging are indeed true, and medical advances are either arresting some of these changes or in some cases restoring function.

Psychological Perspective. This perspective focuses on how we develop as individuals and examines primarily internal developmental processes, including how the environment may shape this internal sense of self or inner being. Numerous concepts form the foundation for the study of development from the psychological frame: ego development, cognitive and intellectual development, moral development, faith and spiritual development, life events and transitions, and relational development.

The ideas within this frame can be organized into three categories: sequential models of development, life events and transitions, and relational models (Merriam and Caffarella, 1999). The sequential models, exemplified by the work of Erikson (1963), Levinson (1986), and Kohlberg (1973), view life as unfolding in major stages or phases. Some theorists tie these changes to age parameters, whereas others view them as bounded more by the resolution of key dilemmas or completion of tasks or responsibilities. In the second category, life event or transition models, particular events or periods of a person's life are seen as driving development—as markers that give "shape and direction to the various aspects of a person's life" (Danish and others, as quoted by Sugarman, 1986, p. 131). Life events may be individually focused—events such as birth, marriage, and death—

or they may affect a group of people such as survivors of a tornado, a war, or a flood. The third category, relational models, have largely been built from the experiences of women (Gilligan, 1982; Jordan, 1997). "The metaphor of the ever-changing web of interconnectedness is often used to describe how women (and perhaps some men) grow and develop throughout their lives" (Merriam and Caffarella, 1999, p. 110).

Sociocultural Perspective. Within the sociocultural frame of development, the social and cultural aspects of our lives are the primary forces that drive growth and change in adulthood. One area this perspective focuses on is the social roles we play, such as that of parent, spouse, partner, worker, and friend, and the "correct" timing of those roles as defined by the societies in which we live. As Neugarten (1976) observes, "Every society is age-graded, and every society has a system of social expectations regarding age-appropriate behavior" (p. 16); these shape the developmental process. More recently a great deal of attention has been paid to the socially constructed notions of race, ethnicity, gender, social class, and sexual orientation as they relate to development (Tennant and Pogson, 1995; Evans, Forney, and Guido-Dibrito, 1998; Merriam and Caffarella, 1999). Bee (1996) argues that sociocultural factors shape the trajectory of the life course.

In taking into consideration these contextual factors, it often is difficult to separate which factor or factors have the greater impact on development, as often they intersect in people's lives. People are always multiply positioned socially and culturally. Therefore, understanding how these various contextual factors influence development is not enough; we must also gain a clearer picture of how the intersections of race, class, gender, sexual orientation, and ethnicity affect how adults develop.

Integrative Perspective. Viewing development from an integrative frame recognizes that adults are far too complex to put in one box or another. In order to fully understand development, we need to look at how the biological, psychological, and sociocultural frames intersect and influence each other.

Although researchers have studied development from this perspective for at least two decades (Perun and Bielby, 1980; Baltes, 1982; Magnusson, 1995), models that integrate all three frames of development are not as prevalent as those that consider just one or two of the frames discussed. In addition, few of these models have been studied empirically; rather, they remain in the conceptualization stage. Often what these researchers advocate is the "need for new 'development-specific' research methodologies to address the more interactive and complex models of development" (Merriam and Caffarella, 1999, p. 133). Although some researchers have responded to this call, such as Schaie (1994) in the area of intellectual development, it is acknowledged to be a difficult task. However, the integrative perspectives appear to offer one of the most promising ways for capturing the intricacies of how we grow and develop as adults.

Looking Ahead

The chapters that follow are organized according to this typology of theories. Each focuses on a particular dimension of adult development and summarizes the major work done in that area, as well as implications for adult education. Although the traditional perspectives are addressed (biological and psychological), we have purposely placed the greatest emphasis on less familiar approaches. Under sociocultural perspectives we examine gender, race and ethnicity, and sexual identity. We have used a different approach toward integrative models, choosing various lenses, each of which incorporates multiple dimensions of development, to view the balance between separation and connection, the role of time, development as narrative, and spirituality. We conclude with a chapter that assesses the state of adult developmental theory overall and speculates on how this work will continue to affect our understanding of adult learning.

References

Baltes, P. B. "Life-Span Development Psychology: Some Conveying Observations on History and Theory." In K. W. Schaie and J. Geiwitz (eds.), *Readings in Adult Development and Aging*. Boston: Little, Brown, 1982.

Bee, H. L. *Journey of Adulthood*. (3rd ed.) Upper Saddle River, N.J.: Prentice Hall, 1996.

Daloz, L. A. *Effective Teaching and Mentoring*. San Francisco: Jossey-Bass, 1986.

Erikson, E. H. *Childhood and Society*. (2nd ed.) New York: Norton, 1963.

Evans, N. J., Forney, D. S., and Guido-DiBrito, F. *Student Development in College: Theory, Research, and Practice*. San Francisco: Jossey-Bass, 1998.

Gilligan, C. *In a Different Voice: Psychological Theory and Women's Development*. Cambridge, Mass.: Harvard University Press, 1982.

Jordan, J. V. (ed.). *Women's Growth in Diversity*. New York: Guilford Press, 1997.

Jordan, W. D. "Searching for Adulthood in America." In E. H. Erikson (ed.), *Adulthood: Essays*. New York: Norton, 1978.

Kohlberg, L. "Continuities in Childhood and Adult Moral Development." In P. Baltes and K. Schaie (eds.), *Life-Span Developmental Psychology: Personality and Socialization*. Orlando, Fla.: Academic Press, 1973.

Levinson, D. J. "A Conception of Adult Development." *American Psychologist*, 1986, *41* (1), 3–13.

Magnusson, D. "Individual Development: A Holistic, Integrated Model." In P. Moen, G. H. Elder, and K. Luscher (eds.), *Examining Lives in Context: Perspectives on the Ecology of Human Development*. Washington, D.C.: American Psychological Association, 1995.

Meacham, J. "Autobiography, Voice, and Developmental Theory." In E. Amsel and K. A. Renninger (eds.), *Change and Development*. Mahwah, N.J.: Erlbaum, 1997.

Merriam, S. B., and Caffarella, R. S. *Learning in Adulthood. A Comprehensive Guide*. San Francisco: Jossey-Bass, 1999.

Neugarten, B. "Adaption and the Life Cycle." *Counseling Psychologist*, 1976, *6*, 16–20.

Perlmutter, M., and Hall, E. *Adult Development and Aging*. New York: Wiley, 1985.

Perun, P. J., and Bielby, D. D. "Structure and Dynamics of the Individual Life Course." In K. W. Back (ed.), *Life Course: Integrative Theories and Exemplary Populations*. Boulder, Colo.: Westview Press, 1980.

Schaie, K. W. "The Course of Adult Intellectual Development." *American Psychologist*, 1994, *49* (4), 304–313.

Sugarman, L. *Life-Span Development: Concepts, Theories, and Interventions.* New York: Methuen, 1986.

Tennant M. C., and Pogson, P. *Learning and Change in the Adult Years: A Developmental Perspective.* San Francisco: Jossey-Bass, 1995.

Werner, H., and Kaplan, B. "The Developmental Approach to Cognition: Its Relevance to the Psychological Interpretation of Anthropological and Ethnolinguistic Data." *American Anthropologist,* 1956, *58*, 866–880.

M. CAROLYN CLARK is associate professor of adult education at Texas A&M University, College Station.

ROSEMARY S. CAFFARELLA is professor of educational leadership at the University of Northern Colorado, Greeley.

2

This chapter focuses on concepts and theories of human aging and introduces current thought regarding the interaction and interdependence of various influences on physical well-being.

Our Complex Human Body: Biological Development Explored

Vivian W. Mott

What makes us so anxious about our own biological development? Why do we strive for cognitive and psychological development, delight in the development of a child's personality, and celebrate moral development and reasoning—but bristle at the thought of aging or developing biologically? Perhaps our anxiety is due to the close relationship between biological development and illness, decline, and death. A biological description of the process of human aging is a necessary but insufficient explanation of human physiology; that is, even though "we can describe something physically, the error is to believe that we have sufficiently explained it as only physical" (DeBoe, 1995, p. 128).

The purpose of this chapter is to examine the complex process of human biological development—aging—from a variety of perspectives. The chapter begins with terms, definitions, and theories used to describe and explain human aging, continues with a discussion of new perspectives on human aging, such as interactions among psychosocial influences, state of mind, and physical well-being, and concludes with implications for learners and practitioners alike.

Biological Development

Three concepts are commonly used to explain how long people live: *life span, life expectancy,* and *longevity. Life span* refers to the perceived upper limit of human life—about 110–120 years. *Life expectancy* is the average number of years a person can expect to live, based on current age. Today, for example, Americans at birth can expect to live an average of 76.1 years.

A female at birth has a life expectancy of 82.7 years, but at age sixty-five her life expectancy is 18.9 additional years; a male at birth can expect to live 75.7 years but has a life expectancy of 15.7 more years at age sixty-five (National Center for Health Statistics, 1998). Whereas life expectancy is based on current age, *longevity* is the expected length of life, which is influenced by a person's culture or by the specific time in history that a person lives. For instance, human longevity is currently longer for Caucasians than for African Americans or Native Americans, and all cultural groups enjoy more longevity at the end of this century than was the case in the seventeenth century. Increased longevity in this century and across many cultural and ethnic groups is the result of advancing medical technologies, improved hygiene and nutrition, and increased awareness of environmental and lifestyle influences on health and well-being.

We also define ourselves by age, but we do it in a variety of ways: by *chronological age,* which is merely the number of years since birth; by *functional* or *physiological age,* which is a reflection of the body's functioning capacity; and by *psychological age,* or how old we feel ourselves to be. Although chronological age is an easily determined and (usually) indisputable number, chronological age is not the same as—or even a good measure of—functional or psychological age. More important, our psychological age (how old we feel) can have a significant influence on functional age.

In Langer's book, *Mindfulness* (1990), she describes a variety of experiments aimed at understanding human aging. Langer became convinced that people can "create their own development rather than being trapped in a pattern that is inescapably played out" (p. 46). To confirm her emerging findings of self-determined functional and psychological age, Langer invited a group of eighty men, approximately seventy-five years of age, to consider themselves as men twenty years younger. During a week-long retreat, the environments of half the men realistically reflected a time twenty years earlier; that is, their rooms included newspapers and magazines, decor, and even videotaped television and audiotaped radio from that era. In effect, the men were asked to "be" fifty-five again in their thoughts and daily activities. The other half, a control group, were asked only to think, talk, and write about their lives when they were fifty-five but enjoyed none of the carefully reconstructed environments of that stage of their lives. At the conclusion of the experiment, both groups enjoyed significant improvements in both physiological and psychological functioning. Their blood pressure, heart rate, stamina, cognition—even hearing and blood profiles—all improved, pointing to the fluidity of psychological and functional age. The experiment further convinced Langer of the fallacy of inevitable biological decline based on chronological age alone.

In the age designations themselves and in how we reach those points in our lives, we age due to both primary and secondary factors. Bee (1996) notes the important distinction between primary and secondary aging: "Primary aging is the basic, shared, inevitable set of gains or declines governed by some kind of maturational process. Secondary aging, in contrast, is the product of environmental influences, health habits, or disease and is neither inevitable nor shared by all adults" (p. 83).

However, Merriam and Caffarella (1999) note that "as one grows older, it becomes difficult to distinguish between the normal or primary aging processes and those physical changes that are disease related" (p. 98). Biological aging brings an assortment of physical changes in adulthood; some begin as early as the thirties, such as weight gain and vision loss, whereas others, such as wrinkles and graying hair, are more likely in the forties and fifties.

Long before these outward changes are noticeable, however, internal changes are taking place. In addition to losses in primarily two of our senses—vision and hearing—other changes that can affect learning and other developmental processes include cardiovascular disease and chronic brain dysfunction. Cardiovascular disease can result in stroke, causing the loss of memory, mobility, and the ability to speak. Chronic brain dysfunction can result from diseases such as Alzheimer's disease or other forms of dementia, or from massive brain damage due to trauma.

Bee (1996) notes a variety of other changes as we age: external changes in the way we look and internal changes in our muscle and bone structures, as well as in our reproductive, nervous, respiratory, and cardiovascular systems. These changes combine to affect many aspects of our daily lives, including sleep, dexterity and coordination, sexual activity, stamina, and cognitive function. All of these changes can have a significant impact on our psychological well-being as well as our ability and desire to learn (Bee, 1996; Marsh, 1996). It is important to note, however, that significantly "less inevitable change or decline [occurs] with age than we had previously thought. And some of the declines we observe, while real, may have only small effects on day-to-day life" (Bee, 1996, p. 84). Yet we are more likely to be plagued by chronic disease as we age, a tendency potentially explained by a variety of aging theories.

Theories of Aging

Programmed or genetic theories of aging, as the names imply, suggest that humans are genetically programmed to live for a certain period of time, approximately seventy-five years, based on a programmed number of cell divisions. This "Hayflick limit," named after biologist Leonard Hayflick, who pioneered the cellular studies, refers to the point beyond which cells can no longer replicate themselves (Hayflick, 1994). Simply put, the higher number of cell divisions the organism is genetically programmed to have, the longer the potential life span of the organism. During the programmed life span, various changes occur—changes controlled by our biological and immune clocks. The biological clock signals puberty, fertility, menopause in women, and ultimately death. The function of the immune clock, which is thought to reside in the thymus gland, begins to decline well before midlife and leaves us with increased susceptibility to illness and death.

A related genetically based concept, the metabolic theory, similarly suggests that all species have a specific and finite metabolic capacity that affects how long an organism can live. Simply stated, the higher the metabolic rate the shorter the life span. In decades of research with chimpanzees, rodents, and other small mammals, caloric restriction has been found to lower their metabolic rate and thus lengthen their life span. Perhaps the same holds true for humans. Ray Walford (1986), for instance, professor of pathology and gerontology in the University of California, Los Angeles, School of Medicine and one of the Biosphere2 inhabitants, notes that an appropriate and well-engineered diet can extend the life span well beyond the commonly recognized upper limit of 110–120 years.

The "wear and tear" or stochastic theories of aging also help explain our biological development and aging. One such theory suggests that the human body ages due to accumulated damage caused by highly reactive free radicals—unstable molecules that have either lost or gained an electron. Cell damage is brought about when free radicals attempt to stabilize through accessing or casting off an electron. Free radicals occur normally as a result of exposure to sunlight and X-rays and are also brought about by diet and normal body metabolism. Although the body can repair cell damage to a certain degree, this ability of the immune system decreases with age. The body experiences decreased cellular function and subsequent disease as a result of cumulative unrepaired cellular damage. Because oxygen radicals are thought to be the most destructive, an increase in antioxidants in the form of fresh fruits and vegetables is a highly recommended means of slowing the aging process due to free radical cell damage (Hayflick, 1994; Medina, 1995).

The glycation theory is another explanation of human aging; it suggests that cell damage is caused by toxic byproducts of human energy production. When glucose and oxygen are burned to create energy, the toxic wastes created interact with cellular membranes, proteins, and even DNA, weakening membranes and reducing the cell's defense mechanism. The process ultimately results in cross-links or bonds between protein molecules or within a single molecule, many of which can cause age-related changes throughout the body. Physicians, nutritionists, and other health professionals stress that many maladies associated with aging—atherosclerosis and hypertension, as well as neurological, vision, and immune deficiencies—are all worsened by high blood glucose levels.

Thus, "from head to toe, from proteins to DNA, from birth to death, untold battalions of processes unfold to create the aging of a 60–trillion-celled human" (Medina, 1995, p. 48). But are all of these processes biological? Although it is clear that adults age differently, there is evidence to suggest that some of those differences may be due to mental attitude as well as to environmental and psychosocial influences. Our mental states interact in complex ways with our physical health, affecting, for instance, drug efficacy and side effects, pain tolerance, degree of disability, and even death

(DeBoe, 1995; Katz, 1998). But questions remain regarding the degree of control adults can exert on these biological changes. Are they inevitable? Or can our minds and daily environments in some way alter the effect of the changes, if not the occurrences themselves?

Toward New Perspectives on Biological Development

Aging is a state of mind as well as of body. According to Murphy, author of *The Future of the Body: Explorations into the Further Evolution of Human Nature* (1992), our state of mind is significantly influenced not only by our mental processes but by cultural and psychosocial factors as well. Murphy proposes an assortment of alternative views of human development and suggests that mental attitudes, culture, and environment exert significant influence on what he terms the "metanormal capacity" to direct our own biopsychosocial development. Similarly, Margaret Gullette (1997) maintains that we are aged by culture in ways that undermine a fuller appreciation of human capacity. She suggests that our preoccupation with aging and decline is brought on by an "age ideology." As Gullette explains, *age ideology* is a socially constructed system of beliefs about biological development, midlife, and aging—beliefs that are deeply embedded in our culture. She argues that not only does society suffer from ageism but an age ideology can ultimately affect not just how well we age but how long we live. Schachter-Shalomi and Miller (1997) are two other scholars whose writings seek to recognize and strengthen the mind-body connection and its relationship to human aging. They practically glorify aging in their book, *From Age-ing to Sage-ing: A Profound New Vision of Growing Older.* The authors propose a radically different model of human development in which life experiences become the catalysts for better health and more positive psychosocial development.

The fact that the mind influences the body is, in spite of its neglect by biology and traditional medicine, one of the more fundamental facts about the process of life. Our ability to maintain an optimistic attitude may actually improve our physical health, assist in controlling pain and other symptoms, and even help us survive life-threatening illnesses. According to Norman Anderson (1998), director of the National Institutes of Health, Office of Behavioral and Social Sciences Research:

> Our beliefs, our emotions, our behavior, our thoughts, our family and cultural systems, as well as the environmental context in which we live, all are as relevant to our health as our genetic inheritance and our physiology. . . . Health science has reached a point where it is no longer accurate to talk about psychology *versus* biology; the mind *versus* the body; or nature *versus* nurture. These processes are inextricably linked [p. 2].

Increasingly, discussions of health and aging such as Anderson's include reference to the mind-body connection, that is, the concept that the mind affects biological development. In other words, what and how we think about ourselves has a significant impact on the way we develop.

The notion of the mind-body connection is not a new one but is a reemergence of ideas and practices from ancient Greek and later Renaissance physicians. An earlier holistic understanding of a complex, dynamic, and interrelated human system

> was almost entirely displaced . . . by the dualistic view of human functioning developed by post-Renaissance thinkers. . . . In this new understanding, mind lost its intimate connections with the body and was thought to operate in parallel with physiological processes rather than through constant interplay with them. . . . The body was assigned to anatomists and physiologists, the mind to philosophers and psychologists [Murphy, 1992, p. 22].

Rene Descartes, to whom the idea of the separateness of the mind and body is attributed, argued that the essences of mind and body merged somewhere near the center of the human brain, perhaps in the area now known to be the pineal gland. Even though he stressed their separateness, however, Descartes suggested the possibility of exchanged messages between the mind and body via this gland. The likelihood of messages from our minds to our bodies is hardly at issue today.

Murphy (1992) writes:

> Our body produces as yet undetermined numbers of messenger substances, some of them secreted by the central nervous system, some by the endocrine system, and some by the immune system. . . . In short, many bidirectional pathways between the nervous, endocrine, and immune systems are being specified now so that disciplines such as immunology and endocrinology that were traditionally separated must work in concert for optimal results [pp. 20–21].

In his hallmark text, *Love, Medicine, and Miracles,* Siegel (1986) explains his use of emotion and imagery to help cancer patients change their bodies and biological functioning by coaxing their minds and bodies to communicate with each other. Emotions let the body know how the patient feels about the biological processes, and imagery or visualization help to bring about desired changes. According to Siegel, "We don't yet understand all the ways in which brain chemicals are related to emotions and thoughts . . . the salient point is that our state of mind has an immediate and direct effect on our state of body. We can change the body by dealing with how we feel" (p. 69).

Chopra (1993) echoes the message that human biology is fluid and changeable and adds his own positive assertion that we "can change our biology by what we think and feel" (p. 4). In *Ageless Body, Timeless Mind,* Chopra suggests that "distressed mental states get converted into the biochemicals that create disease" (p. 17). He explains:

Our cells are constantly eavesdropping on our thoughts and being changed by them. A bout of depression can wreak havoc with the immune system; falling in love can boost it. Despair and hopelessness raise the risk of heart attacks and cancer, thereby shortening life. Joy and fulfillment keep up health and extend life [p. 5].

The point of Chopra's message is that long-held assumptions about the separation of mind and body—about an objectified world—do not accurately represent a worldview that is necessary for health and well-being. Rather, Chopra's premise is based on a "new" assumption that the "mind and body are inseparably one" (p. 16).

Books such as Norman Cousins's *Anatomy of an Illness,* Bernie Siegel's *Love, Medicine, and Miracles,* or Deepak Chopra's *Ageless Body, Timeless Mind* may have been best-sellers, but they were slow to achieve the acclaim of mainstream health professionals. Conventional medicine as we know it, practiced for only a few centuries, is slowly becoming more receptive to an integrative approach to mental and physical well-being, and much of what is considered nontraditional to some has been accepted practice in indigenous cultures throughout much of the world. We've moved from accepting the benefits of biofeedback for control of pain, hypertension, heart rate, incontinence, and even bleeding, to such concepts as immuno-imagery—the use of visualization to boost the immune system in the treatment of cancer and other disease (Weil, 1998). Today, increasingly complex but intriguing terms such as *psychobiology, psychoimmunology, psychoneuroimmunology,* and *psychoendocrinology* emerge first, not in New Age health journals but in resources such as the *New England Journal of Medicine* and the *Journal of the American Medical Association.*

People in larger numbers are turning to complementary or alternative medicine (CAM) for treatment of chronic pain, injury, illness, and disease. Complementary therapies are alternative medical treatments that may be considered unconventional and unorthodox; they include homeopathy, acupuncture, tai chi, Ayur-Veda, macrobiotic diet and exercise, manual healing therapies such as massage or Reiki, and herbal therapy. Rather than viewing illness and injury as an anomaly of some specific aspect of bodily function, CAM is aimed at righting an overall imbalance that is related to emotions, nutrition, lifestyle, or the environment. In their report on alternative or complementary therapies, Eisenberg and others (1993) found that more than one-third of Americans, primarily people in their thirties and forties who are well educated and have higher-than-average incomes, use complementary therapies, often without the knowledge of their primary physician. And although most medical practitioners do not initiate prescribing such treatment, many feel that some of the therapies may be safely used as part of a rigorous and traditional medical treatment plan (Glaser, 1999). Thus, with or without the help of mainstream medical practitioners, people are looking for reasons behind their illness, injury, and disease and then responding to the biological changes in a new, more positive way—a way that challenges the Cartesian notion of dualism regarding our biological and mental states.

Implications for Adult Learning

The foregoing discussion of the complexities of biological development has important implications for adult educators and learners alike. Adults are living longer and healthier lives, frequently returning to the classroom for personal and professional reasons; current medical and educational research suggests that returning to engaging educational environments can actually promote better health. Particularly in regard to their own health, adults are becoming increasingly self-directed in their choice of health care, "more aware of the limitations of current medical technology . . . tailoring their medical decision making according to their own beliefs and attitudes, seeking out options to improve their feelings of wellness and to extend their life span" (Burg and Hatch, 1998, p. 1128). Adult educators can help support this self-direction, as they would any self-directed learning endeavor, by serving as resources, offering encouragement, and fostering critical reflection.

Adult educators should take care not to perpetuate the negative myths arising from an age ideology as described by Gullette (1997). An appreciation of both primary and secondary aging factors will help educators implement appropriate instructional strategies and materials that offer accommodation. An increased understanding of the complex ways in which the learners' environment, psychosocial factors, and mental attitudes affect physical well-being will facilitate an educational climate conducive to learning. And as advancing medical technologies are coupled with alternative perspectives on biological development, techniques and therapies to further improve human health and well-being will be forthcoming. And whereas only a few years ago we may have scoffed at the idea of biofeedback—that humans could actually control bodily functions by their thoughts—now that and other, similar practices are becoming commonplace. Through an exploration and understanding of new perspectives on human biological and aging, we are at the boundary of yet-unimaginable mental processes that may offer different models of adult development and learning.

References

Anderson, N. B. "Mind/Body Interactions and Health." Testimony before the U.S. Senate Committee on Appropriations, Subcommittee on Labor, Health and Human Services, and Education, Washington, D.C., Sept. 22, 1998. Web address: [http://www.apa.org/ppo/scitest923.html]

Bee, H. L. The Journey of Adulthood. (3rd ed.) Upper Saddle River, N.J.: Prentice Hall, 1996.

Burg, M. A., and Hatch, R. L. "Lifetime Use of Alternative Therapy." Southern Medical Journal, 1998, 91 (12), 1126–1132.

Chopra, D. *Ageless Body, Timeless Mind.* New York: Harmony Books, 1993.

Cousins, N. *Anatomy of an Illness as Perceived by the Patient.* New York: W. W. Norton, 1979.

DeBoe, J. "Neuropsychology." *Journal of Psychology and Christianity,* 1995, *14* (2), 126–132.

Eisenberg, D. M., Kessler, R. C., Foster, C., Norlock, F. E., Calkins, D. R., and Delbanco, T. L. "Unconventional Medicine in the United States: Prevalence, Costs, and Patterns of Use." *New England Journal of Medicine,* 1993, *328,* 246–252.

Glaser, R. "Mind-Body Interactions, Immunity and Health." APA Science Advocacy, The Ohio State University Medical Center, 1999. Web address: [http://www.apa.org/ppo/mind.html]

Gullette, M. M. *Declining to Decline: Cultural Combat and the Politics of the Midlife.* Charlottesville, Va.: University Press of Virginia, 1997.

Hayflick, L. *How and Why We Age.* New York: Ballantine, 1994.

Katz, I. R. "Depression as a Pivotal Component in Secondary Aging." In J. Lomranz (ed.), *Handbook of Aging and Mental Health.* New York: Plenum Press, 1998.

Langer, E. *Mindfulness.* New York: Doubleday, 1990.

Marsh, G. R. "Perceptual Changes with Aging." In E. W. Busse and D. G. Blazer (eds.), *Textbook of Geriatric Psychiatry.* Washington, D.C.: American Psychiatric Press, 1996.

Medina, J. J. *The Clock of Ages: Why We Age—How We Age—Winding Back the Clock.* Cambridge, U.K.: Cambridge University Press, 1995.

Merriam, S. B., and Caffarella, R. S. "Biological and Psychological Development." In S. B. Merriam and R. S. Caffarella, *Learning in Adulthood.* (2nd ed.) San Francisco: Jossey-Bass, 1999.

Murphy, M. *The Future of the Body: Explorations into the Further Evolution of Human Nature.* New York: Jeremy Tarcher, 1992.

National Center for Health Statistics. "FASTATS A to Z: Life Expectancy." Washington, D.C.: Center for Disease Control, 1998. Web address: [http://www.edu.gov/nchsww/fastats/lifexpec.htm]

Schachter-Shalomi, Z., and Miller, R. S. *From Age-ing to Sage-ing: A Profound New Vision of Growing Older.* New York: Warner Books, 1997.

Siegel, B. S. *Love, Medicine, and Miracles.* New York: HarperCollins, 1986.

Walford, R. *The 120 Year Diet: How to Double Your Vital Years.* New York: Simon & Schuster, 1986.

Weil, A. *Self Healing.* New York: Thorne, 1998.

VIVIAN W. MOTT is assistant professor of adult education at East Carolina University, Greenville, North Carolina.

3

Knowledge of prominent theories of psychological development facilitates understanding of the journey through adulthood.

Psychological Development: Becoming a Person

Patricia M. Reeves

I'm sitting in my first doctoral course, Introduction to Computers, and thinking about how the graduate experience has changed during the seventeen years since I completed my master's degree. The syllabus, for example, emphasizes collaboration in the acquisition of many practical skills. What a radical departure from previous classroom experiences where the instructor primarily "talked at" the class.

I'm also struck by the diversity in ages of several in the class. At midlife, I thought I would be the oldest, but Alice is seventy-four years old! She tells the class that she is interested in learning how to word process so that she can record her memoirs for her grandchildren and teach friends at the senior center how to do so as well. Bob, who at age fifty-two was unexpectedly laid off when his company of twenty-three years downsized, hopes to learn skills that will make him more marketable in the workforce. And then there's Sally. Recently divorced and thirty-two years of age, she moved here last week without knowing "a single soul." She expresses interest in learning about Internet tools, particularly e-mail, so she can stay in touch with friends and family. What interesting classmates! How, I wonder, can what I know about adult development help me gain a better understand of students who will be participating in this new learning experience with me?

What Is Development?

Implicit in the concept of development is recognition that it is a process, a coming-to-be. Development "proceeds as a form moves from its potentiality to actuality. An acorn and an oak are obviously very different from each

NEW DIRECTIONS FOR ADULT AND CONTINUING EDUCATION, no. 84, Winter 1999 © Jossey-Bass Publishers

other, yet obviously intimately connected . . . the oak is the actuality of the acorn and the acorn is the potentiality of the oak" (Kastenbaum, 1993, p. 113). Movement from potentiality to actuality occurs over time and in the direction of growth and progress. It is not surprising, then, that most conceptualizations of development incorporate the notion of improvement—of "better," more integrated ways of functioning. "Changes in amount or in quality are evaluated against an explicit or implicit opinion as to what constitutes the 'preferable', the 'good' or the 'ideal'" (Sugarman, 1996, p. 293).

Definitions of the term *development* are based on value judgments. In Western cultures, these definitions have a "distinctly individualistic flavour," incorporating such notions as "being able to exercise increasing control over one's life, being self-reliant, fulfilling personal potential and accepting responsibility for one's actions" (Sugarman, 1996, p. 293). This focus on the individual is consistent with the study of psychology—the discipline largely responsible for shaping our understanding of adult development. In the recent revision of their text, *Learning in Adulthood,* Merriam and Caffarella (1999) define *psychological development* as "development that occurs within the individual, whether development is primarily an internal process or results from interactions within the environment" (p. 99). I will explore this type of development in this chapter.

A variety of theories seek to explain how adults develop over the life course. In the first section, I address classical, time-honored theories, emphasizing those that view development from a stage or phase perspective and those that underscore life events and transitions. I will focus on newer theoretical conceptualizations of development in the second section. Many of these theories emerged in response to charges that classical theories depict development as being too linear, neglecting cultural and gender differences and failing to consider other ways of knowing. The third and final section explores the implications that psychological theories of development have for adult learning. Collectively, the theories in this chapter provide a broad conceptual lens through which to view the journey through adulthood.

Classical Time-Honored Theories

Stage/phase theories of development, as well as those that frame development in terms of life events and transitions, are among the most enduring and influential in the adult development literature. I will consider each separately.

Stage/Phase Theories. These theories are particularly popular because they appeal to the human desire for stability and predictability. The concept of *stages* has been defined in numerous ways in the theoretical literature. However, "more commonly in psychological theories, *stages* imply systematic, sequential, *qualitative* changes in some skill or underlying psychological structure" (Bee, 1996, p. 54, emphasis in original). Moreover, "each stage is thought of as being a structural whole, as having its own logic" (p. 54).

Of the many prominent stage/phase theories (Erikson, 1959, 1963, 1968; Kegan, 1982, 1994; Kohlberg, 1973; Levinson, 1986; Loevinger, 1976; Vaillant, 1977), those theories promulgated by Erikson and Levinson have probably had the greatest impact on the field of adult education. Both Erikson and Levinson maintain that stages of development are hierarchical in nature, that is, they build over time and occur in a fixed order. But Erikson, unlike Levinson, does not necessarily link development to specific ages in life.

Erikson's (1959) theory of psychosocial development remains among the most influential of the stage/phase theories, even though many competing perspectives have emerged in the half century since it was first proposed. According to this theory, an individual has a psychosocial task to master during each of the eight stages of life, three of which occur during adulthood. Because healthy identity development over the life course depends on movement in an invariant sequence through each stage, as well as resolution of the task associated with it, all stages add to and influence one another—a process Erikson terms "epigenetic."

Each stage in Erikson's (1959) eight-stage model is identified by a pair of oppositional outcomes, one positive or healthy and the other negative and thus less desirable. A strength is to be gained by the successful resolution of the "crisis" or dilemma associated with each stage. For example, in the first stage of adulthood—intimacy versus isolation—the young adult must develop a sense of "we" that transcends previous immersion with the self. This is accomplished by establishing one or more genuinely intimate relationships; "love" is the strength to be attained. In the second stage of adulthood—generativity versus stagnation—the individual must find a way to support the next generation by redirecting attention from self to others. Successful mastery of this stage results in "care." Resolution of the final stage of adulthood—integrity versus despair—culminates in "wisdom." Erikson (1968) defines *integrity* as "the acceptance of one's one and only life cycle and the people who have become significant to it as something that had to be and that, by necessity, permitted no substitutions" (p. 139). In short, if all previous life stages have been addressed satisfactorily, those approaching the end of life are able to accept themselves as they are.

Unlike Erikson, Levinson (1986) identifies a relatively orderly sequence of periods during the adult years that are age-linked. He "acknowledges a kinship between his periods and Erikson's developmental stages, but sees a difference in emphasis. Erikson's focus is within the person, whereas Levinson's focus is on the boundary between self and society" (Perlmutter and Hall, 1992, p. 296). Levinson views his theory as building on and expanding Erikson's work, not conflicting with it.

For Levinson (1986), development consists of periods of relative stability (structure building) that are interwoven with periods of transition (structure changing). The life structure, "the underlying pattern or design of a person's life at a given time" (p. 6), is the "pillar" in Levinson's conception of adult development. The basic component of the life structure is made up of an individual's relationships with various "others"—persons and groups, institutions and cultures, and even particular objects or places. These relationships give "shape and substance to the life course. They are the vehicle by which we live out—or bury—various aspects of our selves and by which we participate, for better or worse, in the world around us" (p. 6).

Periods in the life structure are defined in terms of developmental tasks (for example, establishing a niche in society and striving to "make it") rather than by concrete life events (for example, getting married). "Each stable period has certain developmental tasks and life issues crucial to the evolution of that period. A period ends when its tasks lose their primacy and new tasks emerge, initiating a new period" (Rice, 1992, p. 338). Periods of transition, which usually last about five years, provide time to "question and reappraise, to search for new possibilities in the self and the world" (p. 338).

Levinson (1986) organizes the alternating periods of stability and transition throughout life into four eras, each with its own biopsychosocial character; three of the four eras take place during adulthood. The first—early adulthood—lasts from approximately age seventeen to forty-five and is characterized as the era of "greatest energy and abundance and of greatest contradiction and stress . . . we are most buffeted by our passions and ambitions from within and by the demands of family, community, and society from without" (p. 5). The second era—middle adulthood—lasts from roughly ages forty to sixty-five. The biological capacities of adults during this era, although diminished when compared with those in early adulthood, are "normally still sufficient for an energetic, personally satisfying and socially valuable life" (p. 6). It is during this time that most adults become "senior members" in their own worlds, responsible not only for their own work and "perhaps the work of others, but also for the development of the current generation of young adults who will soon enter the dominant generation" (p. 6). The era of late adulthood—the last era of the adult years—begins at approximately age sixty. During this time, an individual confronts the self and makes peace with the world. Although his initial research was limited to middle-class American men, Levinson maintains that his theory also applies to women, different social classes, diverse cultures, and other periods of history (Levinson and Levinson, 1996).

Life Events and Transitions. Our understanding of psychological development in adulthood has also been advanced by a second group of classical, time-honored theories—those that view adult development in terms of life events and transitions. Unlike stage/phase theorists, who see human behavior as relatively universal, biologically driven and, in the case of Levinson, age-linked, a life events/transitions perspective underscores individual variability in human behavior. It highlights the centrality of social, or life, events and the transitions they generate as determinants of human behavior. A life event can be viewed as both a milestone that shapes an individual's life and a process.

Many theorists offer a life events/transition perspective but probably best known are the theories of Schlossberg and Bridges. Schlossberg (1987) asserts that there is "no single predictable, universal adult experience—there are many, and they frequently involve transitions" (p. 74). Transitions are the anticipated events, unanticipated events, and nonevents that alter adult lives. Examples of these events include retirement, job loss, and not marrying, respectively. The more the event "alters an adult's roles, routines, assumptions, and relationships, the more he or she will be affected by the transition" (Sargent and Schlossberg, 1988, p. 58). According to this theoretical perspective, transitions, more than chronological age, provide a framework for understanding and evaluating human behavior. Therefore, it is less important to know that a woman is forty-five years old than to know whether she is making a career change, caring for an aging parent with health problems, or newly married.

Whether good or bad, anticipated or unanticipated, transitions provide an individual with the opportunity to "take stock" and "take charge" of life. "They are the themes that trigger adults to learn and grow" (Sargent and Schlossberg, 1988, p. 59). An individual in transition possesses a combination of both strengths and weaknesses. Schlossberg (1987) clusters these potential resources or deficits into four major categories that she calls the four S's: *situation, self, supports,* and *strategies.* By determining the balance of a person's resources and deficits in each of these categories, it is possible to predict how this individual will cope with the transition. Although transitions in life are inevitable, with a timing and intensity that cannot always be controlled, Schlossberg (1987) asserts that it is possible to control how they affect us. "By systematically sizing up transitions and our own resources for dealing with them we can learn how to build on our strengths, cut our losses—and even grow in the process" (p. 75).

Similarly, Bridges (1980) views life transitions as catalysts for adult development. However, he adopts more of a process perspective to transitions than does Schlossberg, viewing them as the "natural process[es] of disorientation and reorientation that mark the turning points of the path of growth. . . . [Transitions] are key times in the natural process of self-renewal" (p. 5). In short, transition is the "psychological process people go through" (Bridges, 1991, p. 3) to come to terms with a new situation.

Bridges's (1991) conceptualization of a transition consists of three natural phases: ending, neutral zone, and new beginning. A transition begins with letting go of something so that the "starting point for the transition is not the outcome *but the ending that you will have to make to leave the old situation behind*" (p. 4, emphasis in original). After letting go, an individual enters the second phase of the transition process—the neutral zone. The neutral zone is the "very core of the transition process. It's the place and time when old habits that are no longer adaptive . . . are extinguished and new, better-adapted patterns or habit begin to take shape" (p. 6). The final phase, the new beginning, is only possible after an individual has let go and spent some time in the neutral zone—the time when "innovation is most possible and when revitalization begins" (p. 6). Bridges shares Schlossberg's position that change is a part of life and that even though a transition cannot be avoided, it can be controlled.

Newer Theoretical Conceptualizations

The explanatory powers of the classical conceptualizations of development, particularly stage/phase theories, have been challenged on the basis that they predicate "normal" psychological development on the lives of white, American, middle-class men—a statistically small group whose experiences may not be representative of others in a diverse society. Some of the strongest charges levied against these theories have been made by individuals such as Edelstein (1997), Gilligan (1982), and Tennant (1997), all of whom highlight pervasive gender bias in developmental theory. They note that the desired outcomes in many developmental theories (for example, autonomy, independence, and separateness) typify the male experience and that the course of female development, with its emphasis on relationships, empathy, interdependence, and attachment, is rarely equated with healthy adulthood.

Belenky, Clichy, Goldberger, and Tarule (1986) trace the origin of their interest in women's psychological development to the work of Gilligan (1982). In the critically acclaimed *Women's Ways of Knowing,* they postulate the emergence of "voice" as central to the development of mind and self in women, and they delineate five categories in the development of women's knowledge: *silence, received knowledge, subjective knowledge, procedural knowledge,* and *constructed knowledge.* Integration of these five categories represents the developmental ideal for women.

Today, concern with women's psychological development has extended beyond the relational work of pioneers such as Gilligan (1982) and Belenky and her colleagues (1986). At Wellesley College, the Stone Center for Developmental Services and Studies provides institutionalized support for the experiences that define the lives of women. The philosophical thrust behind the Stone Center's work is the belief that women's connection or relatedness to others is crucial to their development and identity. "The apex of development is to be involved in a web of strong relationships" (Liddle, 1991, p. 39) that empower and that have empathy at their core. "The deepest sense of one's being is continuously formed in connection to others and is inextricably tied to relational formation" (Jordan, 1997, p. 15).

Challenges to the comprehensibility of classical theories have also arisen because scant attention has been given to the role of contextual or environmental factors in the developmental process. Kegan (1994) underscores the importance of context in understanding adult psychological development and proposes a way of seeing ourselves in relation to the demands of our environment. He refers to his perspective of psychological development as a "theory of consciousness" (p. 6) that can be used to determine the "fit or lack of fit between what our culture demands [its hidden curriculum] of our minds and our mental capacity to meet these demands" (p. 9). Kegan's theory allows for the "personal unfolding of ways of organizing experience that are not simply replaced as we grow but subsumed into more complex systems of mind" (p. 9). Consisting of five increasingly complex orders of consciousness, his developmental perspective accords particular attention to the adulthood stage of life where its "mental demands" call for a "qualitatively more complex order of consciousness" (p. 92). The emergence of fourth-order consciousness is signaled by the capacity for tasks such as setting limits, maintaining boundaries, and preserving roles—tasks that require the creation of a "*relationship to the relationship*" (p. 92, emphasis in original). Fifth-order consciousness is marked by even greater epistemological organization and is a state that few people reach and, according to Kegan, never before their forties. He does, however, speculate that even though the "evolution of human consciousness requires long preparation," the longer life span enjoyed by individuals today will provide more opportunities to "engage the curriculum of the fifth order" (p. 352). (See Taylor's chapter in this volume for further discussion of these theories.)

Implications for Adult Learning

Courtenay (1994), in a critique of psychological models of adult development, suggests that there is "evidence to seriously question their importance in adult education" (p. 145). He concludes that "the extent to which knowledge of psychological development is an 'indispensable ingredient' of [adult education] practice will continue to be debated" (p. 152). Taylor (1996) defends the utility of these models, stating that they provide an "explanatory framework that is not 'tainted' by our experiences nor by our limited self-perceptions" (p. 61). Moreover, she asserts that a "multiplicity of developmental schema allows adult learners a variety of ways to interpret their experiences" (p. 60).

Let's return for a moment to our opening scenario. How can theories of psychological development promote understanding of Alice's situation? Stage/phase theories provide a framework for normative development and offer "a valuable tool for self-discovery" (Taylor, 1996, p. 54). Alice wanted to learn word processing skills so that she could record her life story for her grandchildren. Enrolling in a computer course not only provided a way to "remain an actively involved, as well as creative, agent in the world of people and materials" (Erikson, Erikson, and Kivnick, 1986, p. 319) but it allowed her to indulge her passion for grandparenting, "one of the most positive and vital involvement of old age" (p. 306). Clearly, "integrity," characterizes the final stage of Alice's life. It's interesting to note that in planning to teach fellow senior citizens computer skills, Alice is "practicing a consciousness of

connection" (Daloz, Keen, Keen, and Parks, 1996, p. 216), a critical component of citizenship in the twenty-first century.

Theories that pertain to life events/transitions illuminate our understanding of Bob's efforts to deal with being laid off. Zemke and Zemke
(1995) found that the more life-changing an event in an adult's life, the
more likely it is to be associated with learning opportunities. "In fact, learning may be a coping response to significant life changes for many people"
(p. 33). It is not surprising, then, that a job loss prompted Bob's decision to
learn new skills.

Theories of adult psychological development that honor experiences
characteristic of women's lives inform our understanding of Sally's situation.
A newcomer to the community, Sally wanted to learn computer skills so that
she could remain in close contact with family and friends. Liddle (1991)
reminds us that "women thrive in relationships" (p. 39). The Internet provides a way for Sally to nurture significant interpersonal connections. Also,
her decision, after a recent divorce, to pursue a life and way of being that
she constructs and "owns" shows movement toward Kegan's (1994) fourth
order of consciousness—the development of psychological complexity.

As the experiences of Alice, Bob, and Sally illustrate, the journey
through adulthood is shaped by myriad psychological, social, physical, and
emotional influences. Taken together, these influences provide the context
for a lifelong journey that is uniquely one's own. Theories of adult development provide a "cognitive road map" for this journey—a guide that facilitates understanding of the wondrously complex and exciting process of
becoming.

References

Bee, H. L. *The Journey of Adulthood.* (3rd ed.) Upper Saddle River, N.J.: Prentice Hall, 1996.
Belenky, M., Clichy, B., Goldberger, N., and Tarule, J. *Women's Ways of Knowing: The Development of Self, Voice and Mind.* New York: Basic Books, 1986.
Bridges, W. *Transitions.* Reading, Mass.: Addison-Wesley, 1980.
Bridges, W. *Managing Transitions: Making the Most of Change.* Reading, Mass.: Addison-Wesley, 1991.
Courtenay, B. C. "Are Psychological Models of Adult Development Still Important for the Practice of Adult Education?" *Adult Education Quarterly,* 1994, *44*, 145–153.
Daloz, L. A., Keen, C. H., Keen, J. P., and Parks, S. D. *Common Fire: Lives of Commitment in a Complex World.* Boston: Beacon Press, 1996.
Edelstein, L. N. *Revisiting Erikson's Views on Women's Generativity, or Erikson Didn't Understand Midlife Women.* Chicago: American Psychological Association, 1997. (ED 415 473)
Erikson, E. H. *Identity and the Life Cycle.* New York: Norton, 1959.
Erikson, E. H. *Childhood and Society.* New York: Norton, 1963.
Erikson, E. H. *Identity, Youth and Crisis.* New York: Norton, 1968.
Erikson, E. H., Erikson, J. M., and Kivnick, H. Q. *Vital Involvement in Old Age.* New York: Norton, 1986.
Gilligan, C. *In a Different Voice: Psychological Theory and Women's Development.* Cambridge, Mass.: Harvard University Press, 1982.

Jordan, J. V. "A Relational Perspective for Understanding Women's Development." In J. V. Jordan (ed.), *Women's Growth in Diversity*. New York: Guilford Press, 1997.

Kastenbaum, R. (ed.). *Encyclopedia of Adult Development*. Phoenix: Oryx Press, 1993.

Kegan, R. *The Evolving Self: Problem and Processes in Human Development*. Cambridge, Mass.: Harvard University Press, 1982.

Kegan, R. *In over Our Heads: The Mental Demands of Modern Life*. Cambridge, Mass.: Harvard University Press, 1994.

Kohlberg, L. "Continuities in Childhood and Adult Moral Development." In P. Baltes and K. Schaie (eds.), *Life-Span Developmental Psychology: Personality and Socialization*. Orlando, Fla.: Academic Press, 1973.

Levinson, D. J. "A Conception of Adult Development." *American Psychologist*, 1986, *41* (1), 3–13.

Levinson, D. J., and Levinson, J. D. *The Seasons of a Woman's Life*. New York: Ballantine, 1996.

Liddle, S. M. "The Stone Center: A Visitor's Perspective." *Initiatives*, 1991, *53*, 37–40.

Loevinger, J. *Ego Development*. San Francisco: Jossey-Bass, 1976.

Merriam, S. B., and Caffarella, R. S. *Learning in Adulthood: A Comprehensive Guide*. (2nd ed.) San Francisco: Jossey-Bass, 1999.

Perlmutter, M., and Hall, E. *Adult Development and Aging*. (2nd ed.) New York: John Wiley, 1992.

Rice, F. P. *Human Development: A Life-Span Approach*. New York: Macmillian, 1992.

Sargent, A. G., and Schlossberg, N. K. "Managing Adult Transitions." *Training and Development Journal*, 1988, *42* (12), 58–60.

Schlossberg, N. K. *Counseling Adults in Transition*. New York: Springer, 1984.

Schlossberg, N. K. "Taking the Mystery Out of Change." *Psychology Today*, 1987, *21* (5), 74–75.

Sugarman, L. "Narratives of Theory and Practice: The Psychology of Life-Span Development." In R. Woolfe and W. Dryden (eds.), *Handbook of Counselling Psychology*. London: Sage, 1996.

Taylor, K. "Why Psychological Models of Adult Development Are Important for the Practice of Adult Education: A Response to Courtenay." *Adult Education Quarterly*, 1996, *46*, 54–62.

Tennant, M. *Psychology and Adult Learning*. (2nd ed.) New York: Routledge, 1997.

Vaillant, G. *Adaptation to Life*. Boston: Little, Brown, 1977.

Zemke, R., and Zemke, S. "Adult Learning: What Do We Know for Sure?" *Training*, 1995, *32*, 31–40.

PATRICIA M. REEVES is assistant professor in the Department of Counseling and Human Development Studies at The University of Georgia, Athens.

4

Although women's and men's sociocultural experiences typically lead them to develop into adulthood via differing pathways and with different strengths, the challenge of adult development is one of becoming a fully integrated person.

Gender Development and Gendered Adult Development

Jovita M. Ross-Gordon

We know that women and men differ significantly in behavior, interests, and attitudes. Most of our social structures and mores reflect these differences; they seem to be a universal phenomenon across cultures, and it is clear that the specific behaviors and interests deemed appropriate for men and women are culturally influenced. We see this everywhere, including the adult education classroom. Consider the woman who has recently decided to return to school to complete her college degree but whose choice of major and career options are limited by her notion of herself as incapable of learning mathematics. Or what of the male college student who chooses a program in occupational therapy because it seems more socially acceptable for a man than the nursing program he'd really prefer? How exactly do we explain these gender-based differences?

The purpose of this chapter is to explore how we construct our understanding of ourselves as gendered beings. First I address several theoretical models of gender development, focusing on infancy and childhood. Then I explore the impact gender has on adult development. And finally I examine some of the implications of gender development for adult learning.

The Development of Gender Identity

Gender identity, simply put, is a person's concept of himself or herself as male or female. We will look first at several theoretical explanations for the development of gender identity, then at some of the major cultural influences on this process.

NEW DIRECTIONS FOR ADULT AND CONTINUING EDUCATION, no. 84, Winter 1999 © Jossey-Bass Publishers

Theoretical Models of Gender Identity Development. What are the mechanisms for acquiring gender identity? I will discuss three that are traditional and one that reflects a more contemporary approach.

First, according to classical *psychoanalytic theory,* fear of retaliation from his father causes the boy to separate himself from the mother to whom he initially develops an infantile sexual attraction (the Oedipal complex) and develop a gender identity in affinity with the father. Girls, however, resolve their phallic stage through identification with the mother, who like themselves, lacks the enviable penis. Chodorow (1978) offers a reformulation of this psychoanalytic explanation, arguing that girls, because they are mothered by someone of the same sex, come to define themselves in terms of attachment to others; boys come to define themselves as separate and distinct.

Second, *social learning theory,* which has been widely applied in accounts of gender socialization, views gender identity as formed through imitation, direct reinforcement for sex-typed activities, and vicarious learning from peer and adult models with similar reinforcement (Burr, 1998). This strand of theory provides the basis for socialization theories of gender identity development. Burr also notes that in addition to real-life models, people have a rich source of symbolic models through television, advertisements, films, books, comics, and so on.

Third, *cognitive development models* assume that an individual's understanding of gender may be different at different ages and that the development of gender understanding parallels the development of a person's ability to reason about other aspects of the world. Kohlberg (1966) proposed several stages of gender development: *gender identity*—children are able to label themselves and others by gender, based on physical characteristics; *gender stability*—children understand that gender does not change over time; and *gender constancy*—they understand that gender is constant across time and situations and not contingent on what they wear or how they behave. Cognitive developmentalists also emphasize the development of concepts about gender and gender schema, which in turn influence future observations of the world. Based on gender schema theory, assumptions about appropriate roles, occupations, and traits become associated with gender labels.

Finally, Bem (1993) formulates what she calls an *enculturated gender lens theory* of gender identity development by situating the individual in a social and historical context. To this she adds the concepts of *androcentrism* and *gender polarization,* noting that through immersion in social practices that convey both male privilege and vigilance to male-female differences, the individual (albeit unwittingly) comes to collaborate in the reproduction of male power.

By the time people reach adulthood, however, it is not just the culture that is limiting them to half their potential. It is also their own readiness to look at themselves through the androcentric and gender-polarizing lenses that they have internalized from the culture. . . . In other words, they are limited by their encultured readiness to constantly ask, "Does this possible way of being or behaving adequately match my culture's conception of a real man or a real woman?" and to answer the question with "If not, I'll reject it out of hand. If so, I'll consider exploring it further [p. 153].

These four types of theories together suggest the multiple ways that gender identity is constructed and maintained. Culture also exerts its influence in specific ways, and I turn now to examine that dimension.

Cultural Influences on Gender Identity. The influences on gender identity development in childhood are numerous and pervasive. I focus on three: (1) the parent-child relationship, (2) the school environment, and (3) the persuasiveness of culturally based, sex-role stereotypes.

The Parent-Child Relationship. It appears that genetic and prenatal factors interact with parental behavior to produce subtle sex-role behavior differences even in infancy (Biller, 1993). Numerous studies have concluded that adults perceive and react to infants in gender-stereotypic ways. Infant boys, for example, receive more physical stimulation, while girls are held, talked to, and touched more; and fathers tend to differentiate more between boy and girl infants when involved in play and caretaking (Biller, 1993).

The School Environment. Burr (1998) summarizes research indicating that a hidden curriculum regarding gender is taught in K–12 education. This is done in multiple ways: teaching materials convey stereotypical images of women and men; teacher expectations and interaction patterns differ for boys and girls; and boys command more space than girls, both physically and linguistically.

Culturally Based Stereotypes. Not to be dismissed are the effects of learning through messages, images, and interactions in diverse cultural contexts, including peer modeling and interaction, media exposure, and observations of and interactions with adults in the community. All these factors influence the early development of stereotypes about appropriate sex-role behavior. But does early childhood sex stereotyping diminish as youth approach adulthood? Werrbach, Grotevant, and Cooper's (1990) findings from a study of high school seniors suggest that sex-stereotypic attitudes have not disappeared by the time young people reach high school. Sex-role stereotypes remain powerful influences on gender identity.

Impact of Gender on Adult Development

Although the primary theory on gender identity has been grounded in childhood development, within the last twenty-five years more thought and study has been given to the impact of gender on adult development. I examine this material through two lenses: (1) research on the differences between women and men and (2) research that questions whether those differences are universally true for both genders.

Differences in Development Between Men and Women. Initially, conclusions drawn from the study of men's adult development were stated as if they were applicable to women as well. In response, a wave of research on women's development followed, with initial efforts focused on expanding or challenging existing models derived from observations of men's lives. Two examples of this are the work of Gilligan (1982) and Josselson (1987). Gilligan used original research on women's ethical decisions as a basis to challenge Kohlberg's earlier claims (1966) that women were not as likely to function at level four—the highest in his stage theory of ethical development. Her work suggests that men and women base their ethical decisions on different criteria, with women more likely to demonstrate an ethic of caring and men an ethic of justice. Josselson (1987) reexamined Erikson's stage theory of psychosocial development, with a particular focus on the identity development of women. Using a framework of identity status originally proposed by Marcia (1966), she postulated four potential outcomes of Erikson's identity stage (foreclosure, achievement, moratorium, and diffusion) and sought to determine how women initially demonstrating each outcome evolved over time. Although the degree of emphasis on relationships varied, being able to maintain a sense of connectedness and affiliation with others was crucial for development to occur.

Research That Questions Differences. A second body of work sought to break fresh theoretical ground, using samples that included both men and women or using all-female samples. In deriving a model of "ways of knowing," Baxter Magolda (1992) conducted a longitudinal study of male and female college students. She concluded that there was developmental change both in how students reasoned and in what they valued in the teaching-learning transaction as they progressed through college, and that there were gender-related patterns within each of the three stages, as evidenced by a sufficient number of students to allow gender comparisons. Within the "absolute knowing" stage, men were more inclined toward mastery and women toward received knowledge; at the "transitional" stage, men were inclined toward an impersonal style and women toward an interpersonal style; and at the "independent knowing" stage, men more frequently demonstrated the individual style and women the interindividual style. At the fourth stage, contextual knowing, not enough learners demonstrated differences to substantiate gender-related patterns. At each stage the pattern exhibited by women can be seen as one that is more relational in its orientation.

A final strand of research looking specifically at women's development has focused explicitly on the links between women's development and their social context. Hancock (1985) found that women predictably defined themselves as adults when they took on adult roles, but it was typically not until they experienced a crisis in a significant relationship that they came to feel truly grown up. Contrary to the age-specific models of adult development, Hancock found these crises to be occurring during their twenties, thirties, and forties. These growth-producing crises revealed the discrepancy between the socially derived expectation that others would always be there for them and their own experience that they could only depend on themselves.

Peck (1986) proposed a model of women's development that provided a more complete consideration of the influence of social context on their life choices. In her model the outermost flexible core is defined as that of social-historical time dimensions, conceptualized as including social-historical context, chronological time, and psychological aging. Next comes a bi-directional "sphere of influence" consisting of the sum of relationships, including those of spouse or lover, children, family of origin, identification with particular groups, and even relationships with work. This sphere of influence is said to be characterized by flexibility (the degree to which it can expand to include new relationships) and elasticity (the degree to which particular relationships are responsive to the women's changing needs and motivations). Finally, in the center is the inner core of self-definition, thought to be unique for each woman according to her motivations, personality, and personal concerns but also heavily dependent on the sum of social-historical time dimensions and the elasticity and flexibility of the sphere of influence.

Caffarella and Olson (1993) provide an overview of all the literature on women's psychosocial development, and they note four themes: (1) the centrality of relationships in the self-concept of women across age cohorts; (2) the importance and interplay of roles such as spouse, mother, and worker to the development of women; (3) the dominance of role discontinuities and change as the norm for women over linear sets of expectations and milestones; and (4) diversity of experience across age cohorts. Caffarella and Olson's review and the studies described here point to the dominance of connection over separation in women's lives. This is in contrast to the view of autonomy as the hallmark of adult development that is portrayed in adult development models fashioned primarily from the study of men's lives. (See Taylor's chapter in this volume for further discussion of this issue.)

Universality of Gender Differences Among Adults. It is important to note that just as early adult developmental research has been flawed by overreliance on male samples and understanding of men's life experiences to generate supposedly universal theory, contemporary research based on women's lives can be compromised by claims to universality for all women. Awareness of the impact of social context tells us that whereas the power of gender as a social category will lead to some commonalties of experience among women or men, other individual and social context variables will mediate against universal patterns.

An example of this is offered by Anderson and Hayes (1996). In their study both women and men value achievement as well as relationships, derive self-esteem from similar sources, and struggle with ongoing issues of holding on (connection) and letting go (separation). The authors suggest that men get more satisfaction from relationships than previously thought.

Harris (1995) observes that it is necessary to talk not just about masculinity but about masculinities: "Each subculture has its own expectations for men so that individuals raised within subcultures view the dominant norms for male behavior with different lenses, which filter certain aspects of the dominant masculine paradigm, thereby emphasizing differing standards for male behavior" (p. 163). Based on data from survey and interview research he has conducted, Harris has examined how men from different subcultures view each of twenty-four cultural messages about masculinity. He describes how men from different generations, communities of origin (city, urban, rural), and from different classes, racial groups, and sexual orientations view these messages, as well as the impact of sociohistorical influences on their view of what it means to be a man.

Partly in response to critiques of earlier research by Harris and others, race and ethnicity have begun to receive some consideration as mediating influences on how gender affects the development of men and women. In an interview study of twelve African American women, Goodman (1990) uncovered five viewpoints of self-in-relation; she hesitated to describe them as developmental, but they reveal a progression from a point of view referred to as survivalist (concerned with personal survival and that of the family and a commensurate inability to describe the self apart from social role) to points of view focusing on people pleasing, self-discovery, self-establishing, and mutualism.

Wade (1996) examined the relationship between gender-role conflict and racial identity in black males. He hypothesized that African American men are subject to multiple sources of gender-role conflict, including the following: difficulty achieving mainstream society's definition of masculinity, which may be exacerbated when racism and discrimination place obstacles to attainment of masculine ideals of success and power; competing masculinities—one culture of masculinity developing from a European tradition, the other from an African tradition and influenced by a history of racial oppression; and variations in role conflict influenced by a person's reference group orientation (whites or blacks). Each of the externally defined racial attitudes on the black racial identity scale correlated with one or more role conflict scales. Also, no significant correlations were found between internalization (black identity that is internally defined) and the four gender-role conflict scales. "Therefore, men who hold these attitudes may likewise have an internally defined masculinity and an openness to the strengths of what are stereotypically considered feminine gender role traits" (Wade, 1996, p. 29).

Overall, we can conclude that gender strongly influences adult development. Clearly there are significant differences in the developmental process experienced by women and by men. However, it is impossible to essentialize that experience and argue that all women or men undergo the same process. Rather we must recognize the powerful impact of various sociocultural and historical factors on that process and honor its complexity.

Implications for Adult Learning

Adult education provides opportunities for women and men to consider new life choices, including ones less tied to what society has defined as gender-appropriate roles and occupations. A question for educators hoping to assist adult learners is whether and how to assist their development as integrated, whole beings, capable both of constructing and supporting a self-defined identity and working in relationship with others for the benefit of themselves and others. Having made the professional decision that supporting the development of adult learners is a worthy educational goal, the question becomes one of educational strategies and programs. The following questions need to be addressed in order to craft those approaches:

What kinds of experiences can help men and women understand how their own development has been influenced by gender?

What kinds of experiences help women and men redefine their current goals and aspirations, regardless of fit with socially constructed notions of gender, race, and class?

What kinds of programs and teaching strategies support the developmental growth of adult women and men whose sense of personal autonomy and desire for social connection allow them to act interdependently with others?

With regard to the first question, Marienau (1995) spoke of the benefits to women in an adult degree program who participated in her course on women's psychosocial development in terms of the theme of self-discovery. Analyzing end-of-course comments about how the course content contributed to the students' own self-understanding, she identified six recurrent themes: knowing oneself, accepting oneself, connecting with others, changing perspectives, empowering oneself, and seeking growth and development. The need for men to have similar opportunities is made apparent by Anderson and Hayes (1996) in their discussion of differing rates of educational reentry by male and female participants in their national study of adult development and self-esteem. Speaking of men who followed the "blueprints" available to them as they made choices during young adulthood, two of the four case profiles reflect men who have yet to identify new pathways toward more satisfying lives after finding disappointment in their earlier roles as a former college football hero and as a good student and provider.

Such individuals would also profit from experiences aimed at helping adults address the second question, how they can redefine their goals apart from cultural notions of gender, race, and class. This redefinition of goals is what seems to have occurred for the third of Anderson and Hayes's four male case profiles. This profile was of a man of sixty-four who was nearing completion of a Ph.D. in gerontology, having been laid off from a highly successful career in the oil industry at the age of fifty. Experiences that support adults in making bold decisions run counter to the earlier gender-stereotypic idea that life choices must be ones that enable them to engage in values clarification, as well as in exploration of career options compatible with their personal values and interests.

The third question seeks to identify program types and teaching strategies that support developmental growth toward both autonomy and connection. In describing what they see as teaching strategies that support the developmental growth of adults, Fiddler and Marienau (1995) identify three criteria essential to such strategies: (1) they are transferable to the learner, such that the learner can incorporate them as learning strategies useable in a variety of academic and life settings; (2) they are congruent with gender-related learning modes; and (3) they are geared to characteristics of developing adults. They preface their recommendations for learner-centered teaching with the following comments:

> We advance the proposition that teaching that best supports development offers a learner models for managing learning—inside and outside the academic context, in a variety of independent and social settings, and in relationship with a variety of others and a myriad of subjects. Ideally the models will be rich and varied enough to accommodate the wide-ranging differences among women learners as well as their commonalties [p. 75].

Their statement could be expanded to include male as well as female students. In principle it suggests that program development and instructional strategies aimed at nurturing fully integrated adult development should meet learners where they are, build on their strengths as either separate or connected knowers, and broaden their repertoire both of independent and cooperative learning strategies in ways that enhance their capacity as learners.

An understanding of how gender shapes development offers the adult educator multiple ways to enhance the learning of students in ways that will significantly benefit them. It becomes yet another means that will enable us to facilitate the ongoing development of our students.

References

Anderson, D. Y., and Hayes, C. L. *Gender, Identity and Self-Esteem: A New Look at Adult Development.* New York: Springer, 1996.

Baxter Magolda, M. B. *Knowing and Reasoning in College: Gender-Related Patterns in Students' Intellectual Development.* San Francisco: Jossey-Bass, 1992.

Bem, S. L. *The Lenses of Gender: Transforming the Debate on Sexual Inequality.* New Haven: Yale University Press, 1993.

Biller, H. B. *Fathers and Families: Paternal Factors in Child Development.* Westport, Conn.: Auburn House, 1993.

Burr, V. *Gender and Social Psychology.* London: Routledge, 1998.

Caffarella, R., and Olson, S. K. "Psychosocial Development of Women: A Critical Review of the Literature." *Adult Education Quarterly,* 1993, 43 (3), 125–151.

Chodorow, N. *The Reproduction of Mothering*. Berkeley: University of California Press, 1978.

Fiddler, M., and Marienau, C. "Linking Learning, Teaching and Development." In K. Taylor and C. Marienau (eds.), *Learning Environments for Women's Adult Development: Bridges Toward Change*. New Directions for Adult and Continuing Education, no. 65. San Francisco: Jossey-Bass, 1995.

Gilligan, C. *In a Different Voice: Psychological Theory and Women's Development*. Cambridge, Mass.: Harvard University Press, 1982.

Goodman, D. "African-American Women's Voices: Expanding Theories of Women's Development." *Sage*, 1990, *12* (2), 3–14.

Hancock, E. "Age or Experience?" *Human Development*, 1985, *28*, 274–278.

Harris, I. *Messages Men Hear: Constructing Masculinities*. London: Taylor and Francis, 1995.

Josselson, R. *Finding Herself: Pathways to Identity Development in Women*. San Francisco: Jossey-Bass, 1987.

Kohlberg, L. "A Cognitive-Developmental Analysis of Children's Sex Role Concepts and Attitudes." In E. E. Maccoby (ed.), *The Development of Sex Differences*. Stanford, Calif.: Stanford University Press, 1966.

Marcia, J. E. "Development and Validation of Ego Identity Status." *Journal of Personality and Social Psychology*, 1966, *3*, 551–558.

Marienau, C. "In Their Own Voices: Women Learning About Their Own Development." In K. Taylor and C. Marienau (eds.), *Learning Environments for Women's Adult Development: Bridges Toward Change*. New Directions for Adult and Continuing Education, no. 65. San Francisco: Jossey-Bass, 1995.

Peck, T. A. "Women's Self-Definition in Adulthood: From a Different Model?" *Psychology of Women Quarterly*, 1986, *10*, 274–284.

Wade, J. "African American Men's Gender Role Conflict: The Significance of Racial Identity." *Sex Roles*, 1996, *34* (1/2), 12–33.

Werrbach, G. B., Grotevant, H. D., and Cooper, C. R. "Gender Differences in Adolescents' Identity Development in the Domain of Sex Role Concepts." *Sex Roles*, 1990, *23* (7/8), 349–362.

JOVITA M. ROSS-GORDON is associate professor of developmental and adult education at Southwest Texas State University, San Marcos.

5

This chapter explores how racial and ethnic identity develops and how a sensitivity to this process can improve adult education.

Racial and Ethnic Identity and Development

Alicia Fedelina Chávez, Florence Guido-DiBrito

Racial and ethnic identity are critical parts of the overall framework of individual and collective identity. For some especially visible and legally defined minority populations in the United States, racial and ethnic identity are manifested in very conscious ways. This manifestation is triggered most often by two conflicting social and cultural influences. First, deep conscious immersion into cultural traditions and values through religious, familial, neighborhood, and educational communities instills a positive sense of ethnic identity and confidence. Second, and in contrast, individuals often must filter ethnic identity through negative treatment and media messages received from others because of their race and ethnicity.

These messages make it clear that people with minority status have a different ethnic make-up and one that is less than desirable within mainstream society. Others, especially white Americans, manifest ethnic and racial identity in mostly unconscious ways through their behaviors, values, beliefs, and assumptions. For them, ethnicity is usually invisible and unconscious because societal norms have been constructed around their racial, ethnic, and cultural frameworks, values, and priorities and then referred to as "standard American culture" rather than as "ethnic identity." This unconscious ethnic identity manifests itself in daily behaviors, attitudes, and ways of doing things. Unlike many minority cultures, there is little conscious instilling of specific ethnic identity through white communities, nor is differential ethnic treatment often identified in the media of white cultures. As we discuss throughout this chapter, everyone benefits from the development of a conscious ethnic identity and benefits as well when multicultural frameworks are used in their learning environments.

The purpose of this chapter is to review pertinent racial and ethnic identity literature to better understand how it informs adult learning. First, we define racial and ethnic identity and stress the importance of examining these concepts from a multidimensional frame. Next, we discuss racial and ethnic identity through developmental and descriptive lenses and highlight the strengths and limitations of the models presented. Finally, we discuss implications and share strategies for working with adult learners.

Definitions of Racial and Ethnic Identity

The constructs of race and ethnicity in the United States are complex and difficult to define and frame. Researchers are not consistent in their meaning, which makes these concepts particularly challenging to grasp. To add to the confusion, racial and ethnic identity "transcends traditional categories and has become a major topic in psychology, literature, theology, philosophy, and many other disciplines" (Harris, 1995, p. 2).

The concept of racial identity, in particular, has been misunderstood and contested. Some meanings are derived from its biological dimension (Spickard, 1992) and others from its social dimension (Helms, 1995; Spickard, 1992). As a biological category, race is derived from an individual's "physical features, gene pools and character qualities" (Spickard, 1992, p. 14). Using these features as distinguishing characteristics, Europeans grouped people hierarchically by physical ability and moral quality, with Caucasians as the pinnacle, followed by Asians and Native Americans, and Africans last on the racial ladder (Spickard, 1992). However, looking beyond these characteristics, there are more similarities than differences between racial groups and more differences than similarities within these groups (Littlefield, Lieberman, and Reynolds, 1982).

Today, literary and theoretical manifestations of racial identity are discussed not in biological terms (which may imply a racist perspective) but as a social construction, which "refers to a sense of group or collective identity based on one's perception that he or she shares a common heritage with a particular racial group" (Helms, 1993, p. 3). Racial identity seems most often, however, to be a frame in which individuals categorize others, often based on skin color (O'Hearn, 1998). The use of skin color is one of many labeling tools that allow individuals and groups to distance themselves from those they consider different from themselves (Chávez, Guido-DiBrito, and Mallory, 1996). Racial identity is a surface-level manifestation based on what we look like yet has deep implications in how we are treated.

Ethnic identity is often considered a social construct as well (Waters, 1990). It is viewed as an individual's identification with "a segment of a larger society whose members are thought, by themselves or others, to have a common origin and share segments of a common culture and who, in addition, participate in shared activities in which the common origin and culture are significant ingredients" (Yinger, 1976, p. 200). Ethnic identity seems most often to be a frame in which individuals identify consciously or unconsciously with those with whom they feel a common bond because of similar traditions, behaviors, values, and beliefs (Ott, 1989). These points of connection allow individuals to make sense of the world around them and to find pride in who they are. If, however, positive ethnic group messages and support are not apparent or available to counteract negative public messages, a particular individual is likely to feel shame or disconnection toward their own ethnic identity. Ethnic identity development consists of an individual's movement toward a highly conscious identification with their own cultural values, behaviors, beliefs, and traditions. Ethnic and racial identity models provide a theoretical structure for understanding individuals' negotiation of their own and other cultures.

Models of Ethnic and Racial Identity Development

Models and theories of racial and ethnic identity development have rapidly multiplied in the last two decades as the "melting pot" framework has given way to acknowledgment of a racially and ethnically diverse U.S. population. Most identity development models and theories trace their roots to either the psychosocial research of Erik Erikson (1959/1980), the identity formation studies of Marcia (1980), or the cognitive structural work of Jean Piaget (1952). Curiously, all identity models focus on the psychosocial process of defining the self; some also acknowledge the cognitive complexity of the self-definition process (Evans, Forney, and Guido-DiBrito, 1998; Helms, 1993). The traditional models in both categories (psychosocial and cognitive structural) are stage models in which growth occurs linearly in a stepwise progression, whereas contemporary models describe racial and ethnic identity as a process that occurs over a lifetime.

Racial Identity Development. These models were originally developed primarily for African Americans to understand the black experience in the United States. Cross (1971, 1995) developed one of the first and most prevalent models of psychological nigrescence, a "resocialization experience" (1995, p. 97), in which a healthy black progresses from a non-Afrocentric to an Afrocentric to a multicultural identity. During this transformation, the individual ideally moves from a complete unawareness of race through embracing black culture exclusively toward a commitment to many cultures and addressing the concerns of all oppressed groups. Cross's model is helpful in outlining racial identity as a dynamic progression, as influenced by those in a particular individual's ethnic group as well as those outside it, and in acknowledging ethnocentric and multicultural frames. Grounded in the context of the civil rights movement, Cross's early work is problematic in that he starts from the premise that before blacks experience identity, they are first unaware of their race and the race of others.

Parham (1989) describes cycles of racial identity development as a lifelong, continuously changing process for blacks. He theorizes that individuals move through angry feelings about whites and develop a positive black frame of reference. Ideally this leads to a realistic perception of one's racial identity and to bicultural success. Parham relates black identity directly to white people in a way that moves individual black identity from the unconscious to the conscious. This model clearly delineates that when blacks brush up against white culture and negative differential treatment by others, feelings of difference are triggered and subsequently a consciousness of racial identity is as well.

What is helpful in Parham's model is a sense of progression. In addition, the model outlines a movement from an unconscious to a conscious racial identity. Problematic in Parham's model is his identification of unavoidable exposure to racial difference as the primary trigger for the development of racial identity. Rather, we believe the primary trigger for individual racial identity is immersion in one's own racial group and transference of a racial self through that immersion.

Helms (1993, 1994, 1995) developed one of the first white racial identity models. Her model presupposes the existence of white superiority and individual, cultural, and institutional racism. Finding *stages* to be a limiting concept, primarily because individuals can be in more than one stage at a time, Helms instead refers to the *status* of white racial identity. Her first three statuses outline how a white individual progresses away from a racist frame before moving to the next three statuses where they discover a nonracist white identity. Helms's model is helpful in outlining interracial exposure as a powerful trigger for the development of racial identity. Problematic in this model is Helms's confusion of an individual's development toward a nonracist frame with development of a racial identity. Her premise is that racial identity for whites is about their perceptions, feelings, and behaviors toward blacks rather than about the development and consciousness of an actual white racial identity.

The Cross, Parham, and Helms racial identity models all discuss what we would describe as an intersection between racial perceptions of others (racism) and racial perception of self (racial development). Although our perceptions of others are important and act as triggers for development and consciousness, there is great value in the consideration of racial and ethnic identity for oneself and groups of individuals.

Ethnic Identity Development. These models focus on what people learn about their culture from family and community. In other words, a sense of ethnic identity is developed from shared culture, religion, geography, and language of individuals who are often connected by strong loyalty and kinship as well as proximity (Torres, 1996). Aspects that make up learned culture include rituals, symbols, and behavior that manifest themselves from underlying values, beliefs, and assumptions (Ott, 1989). Models of identity development typically outline commonalities that are likely within a particular ethnic group. We discuss three of these models as representative of this concept.

Garrett and Walking Stick Garrett (1994) provide a descriptive model of Native American identity and worldview. They offer numerous components of Native American ethnic values and perspectives, including the meaning of tribe, spirituality, harmony, balance, and humor. For example, Native Americans who hold strong cultural identification are likely to honor and use elders as resources in their negotiation of life's path. Ideally, within many Native American tribes individuals gain rather than decline in usefulness to the community as they age and develop a complex wisdom to be shared with members of the tribe. Garrett and Walking Stick Garrett's model is helpful in providing some sense of common patterns of Native American values, identity, and worldview. In addition, they contrast each Native component with "mainstream" culture, discuss the conscious nature of Native identity developed through cultural immersion, and provide some implications for working with Native American clients. It is important to note, however, that there can be enormous diversity within any ethnic population, so any model can serve only as a guide to common patterns of ethnic identity.

In her descriptive model of white ethnic identity and worldview, Katz (1989) identifies fifteen separate values and perspectives of white American cultural identity. These range from a concept of time, which is linear and guarded as a commodity, to a win-lose orientation, which is linked directly to the value of competition. Individuals within white, U.S. ethnic groups also tend to value and reward independence and autonomy. Katz points out that individuals who hold these beliefs "obscure" their connection to others and to a shared culture. Katz's model, although not empirically based, offers a more proactive frame than other models, as it is less constructed from a "whites are born racist" framework. This model does not, however, provide a developmental perspective outlining the journey whites experience in forming an ethnic identity. In addition, the Katz model does not address triggers (or their absence) for the development of consciousness of ethnic identity.

Phinney (1990) developed a model describing an ethnic identity process that she considers applicable to all ethnic groups. Phinney proposes that most ethnic groups must resolve two basic conflicts that occur as a result of their membership in a nondominant group. First, nondominant group members must resolve the stereotyping and prejudicial treatment of the dominant white population toward nondominant group individuals, thus bringing about a threat to their self-concept. Second, most ethnic minorities must resolve the clash of value systems between nondominant and dominant groups and the manner in which minority members negotiate a bicultural value system. Phinney's model is helpful in identifying very real triggers for consciousness and in outlining threats to ethnic self-concept. However, it is still missing a discussion of the critical and positive aspect of immersion into one's own culture.

We believe that the resolution of the two issues we outlined may depend on the strength of the individual's cultural experience. Our own experience illustrates this. Alicia, who is Hispano and Native American

(Mestiza), was raised both connected to and in her ancestral home in northern New Mexico. The village of Taos is isolated enough that individuals from these ethnic groups hold most educational, governmental, and business positions in the community. In addition, time, relationships, and other daily aspects of culture are primarily normed on a combined Native American and Hispano culture. For Alicia, this meant that even with many childhood years spent away from Taos, cultural messages within her community were consistent in providing positive, cultural role modeling. Brief time periods in other states with their educational and neighborhood communities also provided more than enough negative treatment for an understanding of the low value placed by many in the United States on these two cultures. These forays also provided triggers in her consciousness of ethnic identity and personal sense of otherness (Chávez, 1998).

Florence resolved her issue of ethnic identity by planting one foot firmly in the Italian culture and through her mama's well-intended pressure, used the other foot "to climb the social ladder out of Italianess" and "rise" to the standards of the dominant culture. Flo's youth was a daily celebration of the intertwined customs, symbols, and rituals of Catholicism, Southern Italians, and South Texans (both German and Mexican American). Often these cultural influences were punctuated by stark contrasts. For example, the Italian Catholic attended Mass every Sunday, helped Grandma Guido roll meatballs for lasagna, and stomped grapes with Grampa Guido for red table wine. At the same time, the German (white-dominant) influence of the South Texan culture led mama to encourage her daughter to stop dating her Mexican boyfriend and join the Cotillion and later the Junior League. Living these contrasts of Italian, German, and Mexican American cultures triggered in Flo a consciousness of ethnic identity and an ability to move in and out of both worlds.

Implications for Adult Learning

It is critical to understand the culturally constructed nature of educational environments and to develop an awareness of the effect of our own racially and ethnically defined sense of self, of learning, and of education. Difficulties arise for many minority and international adult learners when they attempt to negotiate learning environments that have been constructed within an ethnic base of values, behaviors, beliefs, and ways of doing things that is different from their own. Unfortunately, these racial and ethnic manifestations in the learning process are usually unconsciously applied by educators and peers, making them difficult to identify, examine, and modify. For this reason it is important for educators to make "the invisible visible" in their learning environments and in their own roles as educators. This allows educators to then develop multicultural practices.

We believe that learning environments must first be inclusive of multicultural ways of doing, bases of knowledge, perspectives, and styles of educating. Second, a strong learning community must be created that honors, supports, and challenges each learner to be a uniquely contributing member.

Racial and ethnic identity can affect the relationship with learning that individuals have in their learning environments. Most individuals from white ethnic groups have experienced learning that is grounded in their own cultural norms. These individuals have not typically learned multiculturally and are likely to struggle in multicultural educational environments. In addition, their communal skills may be less well developed. Persons from other groups and some white ethnic individuals have experienced learning that is grounded outside their own cultural norms and have learned to some extent to negotiate multiple cultural environments. However, they may continue to struggle even after many years of white-normed education.

Educators can benefit all types of learners by creating environments that balance different cultural norms, such as by designing collaborative and individual tasks, encouraging reflective and discussion activities, and using visual, written, relational, and other types of learning styles (Gardner, 1997). Curricula and activities must be consciously and visibly multicultural to include a variety of worldviews and bases of knowledge. In addition, educators must continually reflect on the influence of the relationship between their own racial and ethnic identity and how they define an effective learning environment and a successful learner. Feelings of comfort and "rightness" for many educators are likely to mean that they have created a learning environment based on their own cultural norms rather than on a multicultural learning framework.

Both racial and ethnic identity affect the experience with and interpretation of relationships with others in the learning environment. As a result of their racial and ethnic identities, learners bring to the learning environment vastly different experiences of treatment by teachers and peers. Members of many minority and international groups bring an experience of consciously having to negotiate and even survive educational treatment of invisibility or negative ultravisibility, lowered expectations, stereotyping, hostility, and even abuse (Vontress, 1996). Many of these individuals have learned *despite* their learning environments rather than because of them. These individuals' bicultural or multicultural experience of life makes it likely that they will possess some level of multicultural skills, an enhanced ability to compare and contrast multiple perspectives, and keen reflective and observational abilities. To cope with others' racial and ethnic reactions to them, however, they may react cautiously, assertively, or sometimes aggressively to teachers and peers. These learners often have a "radar" for sincerity in others' treatment of them that carries into learning environments. Most white individuals, in contrast, are likely to experience and be resistant to ways of learning and doing that are outside the educational norms in which they have been raised. These learners are likely to lack multicultural and self-reflective skills; they are likely to insist on individual tasks and rewards and to discount knowledge bases that seem "alternative."

Educators can create positive multicultural learning communities by teaching in authentic, relational, and self-sharing ways, by encouraging and offering nonjudgmental processing of multiple perspectives, and by facilitating a sense of respectful community within the learning environment. In addition, educators can help learners understand the benefits of developing multicultural understandings and skills for future work and community environments. Attention to these concerns of racial and ethnic identity will greatly enhance the learning experience for everyone.

References

Chávez, A. F. "Weaving My Way: The Cultural Construction of Writing in Higher Education." *Journal of Poverty*, 1998, 2 (4), 89–93.

Chávez, A. F., Guido-DiBrito, F., and Mallory, S. "Learning to Value the 'Other': A Model of Diversity Development." Paper presented at the National Association of Personnel Administrators Conference, Atlanta, Mar. 1996.

Cross, W. E., Jr. "Toward a Psychology of Black Liberation: The Negro-to-Black Convergence Experience." *Black World*, 1971, 20 (9), 13–27.

Cross, W. E., Jr. "The Psychology of Nigrescence: Revising the Cross Model." In J. G. Ponterott, J. M. Casas, L. A. Suzuki, and C. M. Alexander (eds.), *Handbook of Multicultural Counseling*. Thousand Oaks, Calif.: Sage, 1995.

Erikson, E. *Identity and the Life Cycle*. New York: Norton, 1959/1980.

Evans, N. J., Forney, D. S., and Guido-DiBrito, F. *Student Development in College: Theory, Research and Application*. San Francisco: Jossey-Bass, 1998.

Garrett, J. T., and Walking Stick Garrett, M. "The Path of Good Medicine: Understanding and Counseling Native American Indians." *Journal of Multicultural Counseling and Development*, 1994, 22, 134–144.

Gardner, H. *Extraordinary Minds: Portraits of Exceptional Individuals and Examination of Our Extraordinariness*. New York: Basic Books, 1997.

Harris, H. W. "Introduction: A Conceptual Overview of Race, Ethnicity and Identity." In H. W. Harris, H. C. Blue, and E.E.H. Griffith (eds.), *Racial and Ethnic Identity: Psychological Development and Creative Expression*. New York: Routledge, 1995.

Helms, J. E. "Introduction: Review of Racial Identity Terminology." In J. E. Helms (ed.), *Black and White Racial Identity: Theory, Research and Practice*. Westport, Conn.: Praeger, 1993.

Helms, J. E. "The Conceptualization of Ethnic Identity and Other 'Racial' Constructs." In E. J. Thicket, R. J. Watts, and D. Birman (eds.), *Human Diversity: Perspectives on People in Context*. San Francisco: Jossey-Bass, 1994.

Helms, J. E. "An Update of Helms' White and People of Color Racial Identity Models." In J. G. Ponterott, J. M. Casas, L. A. Suzuki, and C. M. Alexander (ed.), *Handbook of Multicultural Counseling*. Thousand Oaks, Calif.: Sage, 1995.

Katz, J. H. "The Challenge of Diversity." In C. Woolbright (ed.), *College Unions at Work*, Monograph No. 11, 1–17. Bloomington, Ind.: Association of College Unions-International, 1989.

Littlefield, A., Lieberman, L., and Reynolds, L. T. "Redefining Race: The Potential Demise of a Concept in Anthropology." *Current Anthropology*, 1982, 23, 641–647.

Marcia, J. E. "Identity in Adolescence." In J. Adelson (ed.), *Handbook of Adolescent Psychology*. New York: Wiley, 1980.

O'Hearn, C. C. *Half and Half: Writers Growing Up Biracial and Bicultural*. New York: Pantheon Books, 1998.

Ott, S. *The Organizational Culture Perspective*. Chicago: The Dorsey Press, 1989.

Parham, T. "Cycles of Psychological Nigrescence." *The Counseling Psychologist*, 1989, 17 (2), 187–226.

Phinney, J. S. "Ethnic Identity in Adolescents and Adults: Review of the Research." *Psychological Bulletin,* 1990, *108,* 499–514.

Piaget, J. *The Origins of Intelligence in Children.* New York: International Universities Press, 1952.

Spickard, P. R. "The Illogic of American Racial Categories." In M.P.P. Root (ed.), *Racially Mixed People in America.* Thousand Oaks, Calif.: Sage, 1992.

Torres, V. *Empirical Studies in Latino/Latina Ethnic Identity.* Paper presented at the National Association of Student Personnel Administrators National Conference, Baltimore, Mar. 1996.

Vontress, C. "A Personal Retrospective on Cross Cultural Counseling." *Journal of Multicultural Counseling and Development,* 1996, *24,* 156–166.

Waters, M. C. *Ethnic Options: Choosing Identities in America.* Berkeley, Calif.: University of California Press, 1990.

Yinger, J. M. "Ethnicity in Complex Societies." In L. A. Coser and O. N. Larsen (eds.), *The Uses of Controversy in Sociology.* New York: Free Press, 1976.

ALICIA FEDELINA CHÁVEZ *is an assistant professor in the Department of Educational Leadership at Miami University in Oxford, Ohio.*

FLORENCE GUIDO-DIBRITO *is associate professor in the Department of Educational Leadership at the University of Northern Colorado, Greeley.*

6

Sexual identity is one of the most important and intriguing, yet least understood, aspects of human development.

The Development of Sexual Identity

Kathleen Edwards, Ann K. Brooks

Sexuality is the source of our most profound private emotional and physical experiences. It has the power to give us both intense pleasure and pain in life. Although we know a great deal about the biological and physiological development of the body's reproductive and sexual function, we are not nearly so knowledgeable about the cultural, psychological, and social processes related to the development of sexual identity.

Sexual identity is a complex concept that involves biological factors, gender roles, sociocultural influences, and sexual orientation in relation to sexual development. In current usage the term generally connotes sexual orientation, and this discussion will focus primarily on sexual orientation as a core aspect of sexual identity development.

Questions about the nature of sexual orientation development sit at the center of a highly politicized controversy that epitomizes the tensions between essentialist and social constructionist perspectives. The attempt to define sexual orientation raises the question of whether we are born with a particular sexual orientation that develops as though we are working from a genetic blueprint (an essentialist position) or whether we develop our sexual orientation as we interact with others in our culture (a social constructionist position). Whether we believe we acquire or are born to a particular sexual orientation has important implications for all of our lives.

In this chapter, both perspectives become evident as we examine sexual orientation within various historical and cultural contexts. Although the dominant sexual orientation in this culture is heterosexuality, much of the literature related to sexual orientation refers to people with gay and lesbian identities. We explore the traditional theories of sexual orientation development, including biological theories, stage theories, and life span models. In addition, we look beyond identity to discuss Queer theory and other

New Directions for Adult and Continuing Education, no. 84, Winter 1999 © Jossey-Bass Publishers

challenges to identity theory. Finally, the chapter concludes with a discussion of the implications of sexual identity development for adult learning.

The Historical Construction of Sexual Orientation

The terms *heterosexual* and *homosexual* were created in the late nineteenth century as scientists began to categorize sexual behavior (Katz, 1995). Ironically, the term *homosexual* preceded *heterosexual* by over a decade. Working within a rational-scientific paradigm, sexologists such as Krafft-Ebing (1894) and Ellis (1933) created numerous categories of sexual behavior in an attempt to capture and bind scientific knowledge about sexuality. Their work focused on pathology and resulted in any other-than-heterosexual behavior being characterized as deviant. These early medical models were based on essentialist assumptions that people's sexual proclivities were biologically determined.

Sigmund Freud was among the first to position sexuality as a core aspect of human development. He identified the sexual drive as the libido, and his psychoanalytic theories hypothesized that psychosexual development begins in infancy and proceeds through a series of stages—oral, anal, and phallic—on the path to puberty (Freud, 1905/1962). Freud also believed that unconscious sexual urges result in repression and inhibitions that frequently lead to adult neuroses. Freud's views on sexuality were considered scandalous in his time, and his work continues to be critiqued on many levels. For example, feminist theorists challenge such sexist assumptions as his description of penis envy in girls. Nevertheless, Freud's imaginative theorizing on psychosexual development has left an indelible imprint on the minds of many people.

Freud also considered the development of sexual orientation in his theoretical frame. In the classic "Three Essays on the Theory of Sexuality" (1905/1962), Freud began with a discussion of what he called sexual aberrations. Freud speculated that the choice of gender as sexual object was related to the resolution of a complex childhood interaction of desire in relation to the mother and father that he called the Oedipus complex. His theory that everyone was polymorphously perverse, or capable of sexual attraction to members of both genders, seems to be one of Freud's few theories that has not gained popular acceptance. What did remain with us, however, was his claim that homosexuality is a case of arrested development on the path to normality, that is, to heterosexuality.

The mid-twentieth century produced a flurry of survey research on sexuality (Kinsey, 1948, 1953; Hite, 1976, 1981; Masters and Johnson, 1970, 1979). Even though all of these researchers produced data to show that nonheterosexual behavior is common, their results seem to have had little impact on what Rich (1980, p. 631) calls "compulsory heterosexuality" in Western cultures.

The American Psychiatric Association removed homosexuality as a diagnostic category of mental illness in 1973. As Fox (1995) notes, this decision "represented an important shift in emphasis in developmental theory, away from the concern with etiology and psychopathology characteristic of the illness model toward articulation of the factors involved in the formation of positive gay and lesbian identities" (p. 53). However, without pathology as a theoretical reference point, a vacuum was created in theories about sexual orientation. It is this developmental hole that today's researchers are attempting to fill with more normalizing and positive models and less pathologically based theories in relation to sexual orientation.

Historically, most research and rhetoric about sexuality has equated sexuality with heterosexuality. The majority of works on the subject have been blindly based on heterosexist assumptions without naming them as such. Yet ironically, the development of heterosexuality as a sexual orientation has been virtually ignored. We have frequently asked what causes nonheterosexual orientation and neglected to ask what causes the dominant sexual orientation of heterosexuality. Only recently has heterosexuality begun to be addressed as a sexual orientation and then primarily by gay and lesbian writers (Katz, 1995; Richardson, 1996). Paradoxically, a lesbian psychologist, Laura Brown (1995), has been the one to call for a broader look at sexual orientation development, including heterosexual orientation, at least in the case of women's sexual identities. Still, much of the conversation about sexual orientation theory centers on other-than-heterosexual identity development.

Traditional Sexual Orientation Development Theories

A number of theories have emerged in relation to sexual orientation development, the work primarily of gay and lesbian scholars. What is important about these theories is that they address sexuality as the intersection of self and society (Brooks and Edwards, 1997). The developmental theories include biological theories, stage theories, and life span models.

Biological Theories. Biologically based studies of sexual orientation primarily focus on etiology. The most promising research relates to neuroendocrinology, which speculates that brain structures that develop sexual differentiation in prenatal and early postnatal development may determine sexual orientation as well as gender (Bailey, 1995). The best-known brain-based work is that of LeVay (1993), which purports to find differences between the hypothalami of gay men who died of AIDS and those of heterosexual men. LeVay's work has generated a great deal of controversy.

Stage Theories. The stage theories drew primarily on Erikson's (1982) work on the psychosocial tasks of identity development and viewed individuals as going through a series of set developmental stages toward the goal of sexual identity integration (Cass, 1984; Troiden, 1988). Cass was the first to include both gay men and lesbian women in her model of homosexual development and is the first to be based on empirical data. It provides a good example of stage theory.

Cass (1984) outlines four stages in her model. In the first stage—*identity confusion*—the individual first asks the question, Am I a homosexual? During the second—identity tolerance—the individual begins to think, I am probably homosexual. The person is willing to tolerate that identity and begins to seek out others of similar identity. In the identity acceptance, or third stage, the person accepts a homosexual identity but may still be guarded in choosing settings in which to be open. In the final stage of Cass's model—identity synthesis—the person's homosexual identity is integrated into the self, and the person is free to develop social relationships with people of both heterosexual and homosexual identities.

A major problem with the stage theories is that they are overly simplistic (Brown, 1995; Edwards, 1997); they assume that men's and women's sexual identities develop similarly. They also fail to address heterosexual development. Nevertheless, they do begin to describe the interaction between the self and the social world in relation to sexual orientation in a positive or at least nonpathological manner.

Life Span Models. D'Augelli (1994) proposes a life span model of sexual orientation that includes gay, lesbian, and bisexual identity development. Taking a social constructionist view, he suggests that identity development occurs in a complex interaction between three sets of variables that change over time. These include personal subjectivities and actions that include (1) the person's feelings and behaviors related to sexual identity, (2) interactive intimacies with family, peers, and intimate partners, and (3) sociohistorical connections that relate to the legal, political, and social norms of a given time and place. The strength of D'Augelli's model is in its flexibility and recognition of the importance of relationship and context. However, his model still does not allow for the complexity and multiplicity of identity.

Discussions of sexual orientation development become even more complex when we recognize that more and more evidence suggests that there may be little or no correlation between individuals' sexual identity and their behavior. For example, a married man may claim a heterosexual identity while maintaining sexual relationships with other men. By the same token, a woman who identifies as lesbian may be sexually active with men.

"Other" Sexual Identities. The depathologizing of gay and lesbian sexual orientation emerged as gays and lesbians asserted a strong positive identity in opposition to the hegemony of heterosexuality. This emergence opened the door to the examination of sexual identities in addition to a heterosexual orientation which, as we discussed earlier, is taken for granted in this culture.

Bisexuality. Although an acknowledgment of dual gender attraction goes back to Freud and psychoanalytic theory (Fox, 1995), there has been a recent proliferation of literature on bisexualities (Haeberlead and Gindorf, 1998; Rust, 1995). One of the earliest scholars to discuss bisexuality in the popular press was anthropologist Margaret Mead. In a 1975 article for *Redbook*, Mead said that "we shall not really succeed in discarding the straitjacket of our cultural beliefs about sexual choice if we fail to come to terms with the well-documented, normal human capacity to love members of both sexes" (p. 29). Mead obviously believed that sexual orientation was culturally constructed, and in fact she privately participated in bisexual relationships herself, as her daughter has reported (Bateson, 1984).

Much of the research available on bisexual identity, such as D'Augelli's model, considers bisexuality as an "add on" to gay and lesbian identity (Fox, 1995) and, as such, a step on the way to claiming a fully integrated gay or lesbian sexual identity. One of the greatest difficulties faced by individuals who identify as bisexual is the hostility from both ends of the heterosexual-homosexual binary. Those who object frequently consider bisexuality as "fence sitting" in terms of sexual orientation (Rust, 1995). Bisexual advocates have responded by critiquing the "monosexism" of both heterosexuals and gays and lesbians. Discourse related to transsexual and transgender sexual identity is also increasing (Bullough, Bullough, and Elias, 1997). As the discussion of sexual identity continues to grow, it will be interesting to see what other aspects of sexuality become storied that are currently silent or invisible.

Beyond Identity

In spite of history's attempt to first pathologize gay and lesbian sexuality and then to distinguish it clearly from other enactments of sexuality, the truth may be that it is not possible to categorize sexuality so easily. Developmental models and clear distinctions demarcating one sexual identity or orientation may be too confining for the ways in which humans grow into and enact sexuality. The complexity and multiplicity of sexuality may exceed either developmental or sexual identity theory.

Differences in cultural understandings and enactments of sexuality also challenge attempts to universalize a psychology or categories of sexuality. For example, we suspect that the married, working-class Afro-Surinamese women who participate in sexual relationships, or "mati work," with women (Wekker, 1999) as well might be stunned to find themselves labeled as lesbian or bisexual in Western culture. Vance reminds us of the dangers of such cross-cultural theorizing: "Because a sexual act does not carry with it a universal social meaning, it follows that the relationship between sexual acts and sexual identities is not a fixed one, and it is projected from the observer's time and place to others at great peril" (Vance, 1989, as quoted in Wekker, 1999, p. 119).

Queer Theory

In response to an increasing recognition of the multiplicities of human sexual meanings and enactments possible, Queer theory has evolved. Its original purpose was to problematize the heterosexual-homosexual binary. Jagose (1996) notes that "queer is less an identity than a critique of identity"

(p. 131). According to Halperin (1995), "Queer is by definition whatever is at odds with the normal, the legitimate, the dominant" (p. 62).

The term *Queer theory* was first used by de Lauretis (1991) in editing a special journal issue related to gay and lesbian sexualities. Perhaps one of the greatest influences on Queer theory was French philosopher Michel Foucault, even though he had little to say about gay and lesbian sexuality specifically. Foucault (1978, 1980) positioned sexuality as a socially constructed and regulated discourse with profound implications for power, knowledge, and pleasure. In Foucault's (1980) view, power does not simply weigh like a force that says no but also runs through and produces knowledge and language. Knowledge and language, in turn, produce our sense of ourselves and others and the limitations we put on our own behavior.

Others such as Butler (1993), Fuss (1991), and Sedgewick (1990) have continued to call into question the heterosexual-homosexual binary and its meanings in our world. Seidman (1996) argues that proponents of Queer theory "take as central its challenge to the assumption of a unified homosexual or heterosexual identity" (p. 11).

Not all gay and lesbian activists welcome the challenge Queer theory represents to a unified sexual identity around which to organize politically. Wolfe and Penelope (1993) point out the historical construction of sexuality and sexual identity:

> We live in the postmodernist, poststructuralist (and, some would say, postfeminist) era during a period when the term Lesbian is problematic, even when used nonpejoratively by a self-declared Lesbian. . . . In one hundred short years, German sexologists have "appeared" Lesbians in order to pathologize us and French poststructuralists have "disappeared" us in order to deconstruct sex and gender categories and to "interrogate" the subject [p. 1].

Still, Queer theory has the potential to disrupt and challenge the nature of our cultural assumptions about the development of identity, sexuality, and sexual identity. Drawing on this potential, Brooks and Edwards (1997) studied women's sexual identity development. Working specifically with Foucault's notion of language as power-infused, they identified four categories of narrative by which women constructed their sexual identities:

1. *Dominant narrative.* The dominant narrative for a successful woman was to "get married and have children."
2. *Counter narrative.* The gay and lesbian narrative was placed in direct opposition to the dominant narrative.
3. *Shadow narrative.* Stories of sexual and physical abuse were the shadow narrative to the dominance of heterosexuality.
4. *Silent narrative.* Much of women's experience of sexuality was simply unstoried. It exceeded the language and social space to discuss women's lived experience. Example of silent narratives in this group included

"I'm too smart, too big," "I don't fit in," "sex is boring," and "marriage is the end of life."

This study is consistent with Queer theory's emphasis on the socially constructed and fluid nature of sexual identities.

Implications for Adult Learning

Sexuality is a source of significant learning and experience for adults. Long ignored as an adult education issue, sexual identity has the potential to open up new possibilities of learning for adults. Learning more about our sexual identities can create new knowledge about ourselves, about our differences, about our own humanness, and even about how learning is created or suppressed in our societies.

The discussion of sexuality has long belonged to either scholars or commercial interests. In that sense, the human experience of sexuality has remained undiscussable in everyday life. By breaking the silence that has traditionally surrounded sexuality, the conversation about sexual identity creates space for new voices. Even the language of "coming out" employed to describe the process of identifying as gay or lesbian implies the breaking of silence and movement from the invisible to the visible. Certainly there has been a dramatic increase in the inclusion of gay and lesbian voices in the conversation about sexuality over the past twenty years. And those conversations have opened the door to additional identifications of difference. For example, literature about bisexuality and transgendered persons has proliferated greatly just in the last five years. Who knows what other sexual differences we are currently blind to that may be important to understand in the future?

The power of language and discourse to privilege or marginalize is particularly noticeable in relation to sexual orientation because it is an otherwise invisible difference between people that is dependent on the speech act for its identification. The importance of language is especially evident in the efforts that have been made to suppress conversation about gay and lesbian sexual identities. Certainly the United States military policy of "Don't ask, don't tell" in relation to sexual orientation reflects the use of silence as a strategy to suppress. As Foucault notes, "There is not one but many silences, and they are an integral part of the strategies that underlie and permeate discourses" (1978, p. 27). It is through dialogue that differences can be identified and understanding developed. Adult educators have a unique opportunity to create conversations about sexual identity in the adult classroom. As a site of learning and a site of difference, sexual identity discussions can enrich our education of the whole person. Dialogue may also lead to a richer language of diversity in relation to sexual identity.

Britzman (1998) describes difference "as the only condition of possibility for community" (p. 86). The inclusion of sexual differences in our learning communities can contribute to our search for knowledge. Once we cease to privilege what Spivak (1995, p. 153) calls "exorbitant normality" in all aspects of our culture, whether that normalcy resides in the sameness of class, race, gender, nationality, or sexual orientation, our potential for learning and community accelerates. The learning communities of the future will be built on the mosaic of difference. Sexual identity is an important site of difference and development and consequently is an opportunity for important learning.

References

Bailey, J. M. "Biological Perspectives on Sexual Orientation." In A. R. D'Augelli and C. J. Patterson (eds.), *Lesbian, Gay, and Bisexual Identities over the Lifespan: Psychological Perspectives.* New York: Oxford University Press, 1995.

Bateson, C. M. *With a Daughter's Eye: A Memoir of Margaret Mead and Gregory Bateson.* New York: Morton, 1984.

Britzman, D. P. *Lost Subjects, Contested Objects: Toward a Psychoanalytic Inquiry of Learning.* Albany, N.Y.: SUNY Press, 1998.

Brooks, A. K., and Edwards, K. A. "Narratives of Women's Sexual Identity Development: A Collaborative Inquiry with Implications for Rewriting Transformative Learning Theory." Proceedings of the 38th Annual Adult Education Research Conference, Stillwater, Okla., 1997.

Brown, L. S. "Lesbian Identities: Concepts and Issues." In A. R. D'Augelli, and C. J. Patterson (eds.), *Lesbian, Gay, and Bisexual Identities over the Lifespan: Psychological Perspectives.* New York: Oxford University Press, 1995.

Bullough, B., Bullough, V., and Elias, J. *Gender Blending.* Amherst, N.Y.: Prometheus Books, 1997.

Butler, J. P. *Bodies That Matter: On the Discursive Limits of "Sex."* New York: Routledge, 1993.

Cass, V. C. "Homosexual Identity Formation: Testing a Theoretical Model." *Journal of Sex Research,* 1984, 20, 143–167.

D'Augelli, A. "Lesbian and Gay Development: Steps Toward an Analysis of Lesbians' and Gay Men's Lives." In B. Greene and G. M. Herek (eds.), *Lesbian and Gay Psychology: Theory, Research and Clinical Application.* Thousand Oaks, Calif.: Sage, 1994.

de Lauretis, T. "Queer Theory: Lesbian and Gay Sexualities." *Differences: A Journal of Feminist Cultural Studies,* 1991, 3, iii–xviii, 2.

Edwards, K. A. "Troubling Transformations: A Collaborative Inquiry into Women's Learning Experiences in the Construction and Reconstruction of Identities." Unpublished doctoral dissertation, University of Texas at Austin, 1997.

Ellis, H. *Psychology of Sex: A Manual for Students.* New York: Emerson Books, 1933.

Erikson, E. H. *The Life Cycle Completed.* New York: Norton, 1982.

Foucault, M. *The History of Sexuality Vol. 1: An Introduction.* New York: Random House, 1978.

Foucault, M. *Power/Knowledge: Selected Interviews and Other Writings.* New York: Pantheon Books, 1980.

Fox, R. C. "Bisexual Identities." In A. R. D'Augelli and C. Patterson (eds.), *Lesbian, Gay, and Bisexual Identities over the Lifespan: Psychological Perspectives.* New York: Oxford University Press, 1995.

Freud, S. *Three Essays on the Theory of Sexuality* (trans. and rev. by J. Strachey). New York: Basic Books, 1905/1962.

Fuss, D. *Inside/Out: Lesbian Theories, Gay Theories.* New York: Routledge, 1991.

Haeberlead, E. J., and Gindorf, R. (eds.). *Bisexualities: The Ideology and Practice of Sexual Contact with Both Men and Women.* New York: Continuum, 1998.

Halperin, D. M. *Saint Foucault: Towards a Gay Hagiography.* New York: Oxford University Press, 1995.

Hite, S. *The Hite Report: A Nationwide Study of Female Sexuality.* New York: Macmillan, 1976.

Hite, S. *The Hite Report on Male Sexuality.* New York: Knopf, 1981.

Jagose, A. R. *Queer Theory: An Introduction.* New York: New York University Press, 1996.

Katz, J. N. *The Invention of Heterosexuality.* New York: Plume/Penguin Books, 1995.

Kinsey, A. C., Pomeroy, W. B, and Martin, C. E. *Sexual Behavior in the Human Male.* Philadelphia: Saunders, 1948.

Kinsey, A. C., Pomeroy, W. B., Martin, C. E., and Gebhard, P. H. *Sexual Behavior in the Human Female.* Philadelphia: Saunders, 1953.

Krafft-Ebing, R. *Psychopathia Sexualis* (C. H. Chaddock, trans.). Philadelphia: Saunders, 1894.

LeVay, S. *The Sexual Brain.* Cambridge: MIT Press, 1993.

Masters, W. H., and Johnson, V. E. *Human Sexual Inadequacy.* Boston: Little, Brown, 1970.

Masters, W. H., and Johnson, V. E. *Homosexuality in Perspective.* Boston: Little, Brown, 1979.

Mead, M. "Bisexuality: What's It All About?" *Redbook,* January, 1975.

Rich, A. "Compulsory Heterosexuality and Lesbian Existence." *Signs: Journal of Women in Culture and Society,* 1980, 5, 631–660.

Richardson, D. (ed.). *Theorizing Heterosexuality: Telling It Straight.* Buckingham, M.K.: Open University Press, 1996.

Rust, P. C. *Bisexuality and the Challenge to Lesbian Politics: Sex, Loyalty, and Revolution.* New York: New York University Press, 1995.

Sedgwick, E. K. *Epistemology of the Closet.* Berkeley and Los Angeles: University of California Press, 1990.

Seidman, S. *Queer Theory/Sociology.* Cambridge, Mass.: Blackwell, 1996.

Spivak, G. C. "Acting Bits/Identity Talk." In K. A. Appiah and H. L. Gates, Jr. (eds.), *Identities.* Chicago: University of Chicago Press, 1995.

Troiden, R. R. *Gay and Lesbian Identity: A Sociological Analysis.* Dix Hills, N.Y.: General Hall, 1988.

Vance, C. S. (ed.). *Pleasure and Danger: Exploring Female Sexuality.* London: Pandora Press, 1989.

Wekker, G. "What's Identity Got to Do with It? Rethinking Identity in Light of the Mati Work in Suriname." In E. Blackwood and S. E. Wieringa (eds.), *Female Desires: Same-Sex Relations and Transgender Practices Across Cultures.* New York: Columbia University Press, 1999.

Wolfe, S. J., and Penelope, J. (eds.). *Sexual Practice, Texual Theory: Lesbian Cultural Criticism.* Cambridge, Mass.: Blackwell, 1993.

ANN K. BROOKS is associate professor in the Adult and Organizational Learning Program, University of Texas, Austin.

KATHLEEN EDWARDS is a lecturer in the Adult and Organizational Learning Program, University of Texas, Austin.

Striking a balance between the twin needs of separation and connection is an ongoing challenge for developing adults and for theorists of that developmental process.

Development as Separation and Connection: Finding a Balance

Kathleen Taylor

"I don't have a life," Alice Koller (1981) writes in despair. Her journal, *An Unknown Woman*, begins: "I'm just using up a number of days somehow" (p. 1). The realization that she has no sense of self that is not derived from others has brought her to the limits of her endurance. "Turn a pair of eyes on me and instantly I begin looking into them for myself. I seem to believe there is no Me except in other eyes. I am what I see in your eyes, whoever you are" (p. 113).

Unwilling to go on living if she cannot establish a sense of self that she recognizes as her own, she spends a winter in a remote area of Nantucket trying to decide "what a feeling is . . . what it is to choose something, how I can have purposes that are my own" (p. 170). Koller was thirty-seven and single when she wrote the journal that documents her painful and ultimately successful journey toward self-definition. She had completed her Ph.D. in philosophy from Harvard. How can a mature adult with such intellectual and academic accomplishments think that she cannot call her life, her feelings, and her decisions her own?

Alice Koller is a dramatic example of a perplexing problem in adult developmental theory. On the one hand, as we develop there is the need to separate from others, constructing an identity that is clearly our own. On the other hand, there is the need to be connected to others, to see ourselves in relation to them and as part of a larger whole. How exactly do we strike a balance between these two apparently opposing drives? Koller represents someone whose life is terribly out of balance in this regard. She has no sense of herself as a distinct and separate being. Instead, she knows who she is only in relation to others and therefore experiences herself as less than

New Directions for Adult and Continuing Education, no. 84, Winter 1999 © Jossey-Bass Publishers

whole. Her task that winter in Nantucket was to discover how to define herself in her own terms and see herself through her own eyes.

Although the clarity and depth of her self-analysis may make her situation sound unique, adult development theorists tell us her search is, in fact, a universal one. Erikson (1959) emphasized separation and individuation in the developmental process, and his work set the parameters for much of the developmental theory that followed. Early writings on women's development (Gilligan, 1982; Miller, 1976), by contrast, questioned the saliency of these models for women and emphasized instead the importance of connection. More recently theorists such as Peck (1986), Kegan (1982, 1994), and the scholars at the Stone Center (Jordan and others, 1991; Miller and Stiver, 1997; Bergman and Surrey, 1997) have put forward models of development that seek to represent the need for both separation and connection in the developmental process. My task in this chapter is to examine how the tension between separation and connection is explored, focusing particularly on theories that attempt to reconcile the tension. I will then examine implications of this tension as it may inform our practice as adult educators.

Development as Separation Versus Connection

Erikson (1959), who was among the first to systematically explore development in adulthood, offers a complex theory of psychosocial development in which the person, over the course of the life span, confronts a series of dilemmas that must be resolved. These occur as the person matures and takes on new social roles; movement from one stage to the next is prompted largely by cultural expectations tied to chronological age rather than on the readiness of the person to deal with each successive challenge. Erikson expresses these challenges in terms of polarities—trust versus mistrust, industry versus inferiority, and so on, for a total of eight stages. Challenges that are not resolved successfully at the normative age for that dilemma continue to affect the individual's development in successive stages.

Of central interest to us are two polarities that confront young adults. The first of these, Erikson says, is identity versus role confusion. In order to establish their own identity, persons facing this dilemma must define themselves as separate from others. As Bee (1996) notes, this actually involves multiple linked identities—occupational, gender, political, and religious, among others. As for the second adult dilemma, intimacy versus isolation, Erikson (1959, p. 101) argues that "it is only after a reasonable sense of identity has been established that real intimacy with the other sex (or, for that matter, with any other person or even with oneself) is possible." For Erikson, separation precedes connection, and a separate identity is essential for healthy connection to be achieved.

A major critique of Erikson's work and of others who built on his foundation is that his research reflects male experience. Gilligan (1982), in her work on women's moral development, offered evidence that these norms were not universal. She describes women's experience as being marked by connection and expressed by care for others. Women experienced themselves as part of a web of relationships that both nurtured and defined them. For example, in terms of moral decision making, women were more likely than men to take into account people's feelings and needs (morality of care), whereas men were more likely to base their moral decisions on abstract principles (morality of justice). Gilligan further argues that, for women at least, identity is not forged separate from others but is a process that proceeds in connection with others.

Development as Separation and Connection

A number of theorists seek to represent development as involving both separation and connection. I will highlight three of these: Peck, the scholars at the Stone Center, and Kegan.

Peck. Women's need for attachment and their potential "loss of self" within those connections were salient factors in Peck's (1986) description of "the process of self-definition in a woman's adult experience" (p. 277). In Peck's model, women's *identity* is depicted as funnel-shaped, expanding as she grows and develops. However, the funnel is placed within a cylinder—the social-historical time dimension—which may contract or expand. In the 1950s for example, postwar conservatism reversed women's wartime gains in social and economic freedoms. This constriction no doubt affected Alice Koller, who wrote her journal in 1961. By contrast, the late 1970s were a time of expansion, as the women's movement supported greater personal and professional opportunities for women.

All of this structure, however, rests on the *sphere of influence,* which is the "relational" factor of this model and describes how family, work relationships, and social-cultural identifications contribute to a woman's sense of self. Flexibility is a salient feature of the sphere of influence. "Lack of elasticity," Peck writes, "forces a woman to weigh the impact of any developmental changes against the possible loss of relationships key to her self-definition" (p. 280). Women must therefore exert constant vigilance in order to both maintain attachment and achieve separation. A major contribution of Peck's model is its integration of Gilligan's (1982) claim for relationships as a positive, ongoing factor in women's development rather than as a symptom of their inability to achieve identity through autonomy.

Stone Center. The therapists and educators who met under the aegis of the Stone Center at Wellesley College (Jordan and others, 1991; Miller and Stiver, 1997; Bergman and Surrey, 1997) proposed yet another model: women's "growth in connection." Jordan and her colleagues (1991) call for "new models of self that can encompass both the sense of coherent separateness and meaningful connection as emergent structures throughout the life span" (p. 79). This feminist interpretation of psychological theory and clinical practice focuses on relational growth as the "organizing factor in women's lives" (p. 1). These authors challenge traditional psychological definitions of self, and propose instead the notion of a *relational self*—one that depends on

(1) an interest in and attention to the other person(s), which form the base for the emotional connection and the ability to empathize with the other(s); (2) the expectation of a mutual empathic process where the sharing of experience leads to a heightened development of self and others; and (3) the expectation of interaction and relationship as a process of mutual sensitivity and mutual responsibility that provides the stimulus for the growth of empowerment and self-knowledge. Thus the self develops in the context of relationships, rather than as an isolated or separated autonomous individual [pp. 58–59].

In this view, empathy and connection are ongoing, essential motifs in women's development and not something to be grown out of or transcended.

Empathy is a major focus of the Stone Center's writings. Quoting Shafer (1959), Jordan and her colleagues (1991, p. 29) define *empathy* as "the inner experience of sharing in and comprehending the momentary psychological state of another person." At first this seems an odd way to try to understand someone else. On reflection, however, how else can we try to understand what is going on in someone else's mind and body? They may tell us, as best they can, but we can never experience what they are thinking or feeling in exactly the way they are thinking or feeling it. So, for the most part unconsciously, we use our own experiences and feelings as a guide. Jordan (1991) also describes a "resolution period in which one regains a sense of separate self that understands what has just happened" (p. 29) in which we relinquish the perspectives of the other person to which we have surrendered and return to our own. But she also points out that this may not necessarily follow. Some people exhibit "empathic failure," that is, they are so permeable to others' feelings that they cannot keep from identifying with them (p. 76). This was Alice Koller's experience. She had turned others into mirrors for herself and had unconsciously "chosen to believe what they see rather than what I see," even about herself (Koller, 1981, p. 84). For empathy to work, there has to be both ego flexibility (to connect with the other) and ego strength (to return to oneself). "If either relaxation or restructuring of the ego boundaries is impaired, empathy will suffer" (Jordan, 1991, p. 29).

Kegan. The developmental model that Kegan (1994) offers us describes the two "fundamental longings" of human experience as "to be next to, a part of, included, connected [and] to be distinct, to experience one's agency and the self-chosenness of one's initiatives" (p. 221). According to Kegan, the crucial issue is how we construct the self that desires interpersonal intimacy, as this construction changes at different points in our journey of development.

For Kegan, development is a process of transformation of consciousness. He has identified five possible transformations (or orders of consciousness) throughout the life span; two are associated with childhood and three with adulthood. I will not describe the transformations of childhood but will examine the two most common transformations of adulthood. The first of these is the move *into* adult consciousness (at the end of psychological adolescence). The second is the transformation of that perspective and is what most people associate with midlife change.

Third-order consciousness—the move into adult consciousness—is most easily described by contrasting it with what it transforms. Teen-agers tend to value others extrinsically, that is, for what they can provide. They make ethical and moral decisions based on their own needs and desires, and they limit their behaviors (*if* they do) based on the likelihood of getting caught or other unpleasant repercussions. However, providing there are adequate developmental supports, by the end of adolescence they value others intrinsically, for the connection they represent. They make moral and ethical decisions that take others' needs and wishes into account, and they behave with awareness of others' feelings and experience guilt when they fail to do so. This development to third-order consciousness is in some measure what society considers to be growing up.

If we construct that self according to the dictates of third-order consciousness, we are unable to distinguish among our feelings, other's feelings, and who we are. This is the position of Alice Koller at the beginning of her journey. The more developed person, however, who is approaching fourth-order consciousness, *has* feelings rather than is *had by* them. As a result, he or she is aware of and can act on choices rather than being at the mercy of imperatives. In either instance, however, it is important to remember that both orders of consciousness are part of everyone's developmental process. In short, Kegan's theory incorporates both separation and connection as fundamental to the developmental process. His complex model offers one of the most useful ways to conceptualize the developmental interplay of these fundamental human drives.

Separation and Connection in an Educational Context

To explore further this developmental scheme for our work as educators, I will examine the experiences of two adult students I recently had in class, Patrick and Betty. For Patrick, being back in college at thirty-eight was the fulfillment of a dream—his dream of completing the degree that life circumstances had caused him to abandon nearly twenty years earlier. Yet, here he was, at the beginning of the fourth week of class, explaining why he had not done the first major assignment. He had, he said, spent a miserable weekend in front of his computer. It was not so much the difficulty of the task that stymied him but his feeling of concern for his next-door neighbor, who was moving, and to whom Patrick had offered help before he started my class. "I just about dropped out this weekend," Patrick said. "I knew you were expecting this assignment, but I'm the kind of guy who *has* to be there when people need me. I told Sam he could borrow my truck, and I sent my son over to help him with loading and unloading. But it just about killed me [his tone clearly showing the depths of his feeling] that I couldn't be there for him. If school is going to mean I can't be there for my friends, I don't think I can do it."

Patrick's level of empathy approaches the "boundary problems" for which women have been indicted in so much of the psychological literature. He feels he *must* respond to his friend's need (and the needs of as-yet-unnamed friends who may call on him), regardless of his commitment to himself to finish his degree. The fact that Patrick did not actually go to help his friend but sat in front of the computer (albeit feeling miserable) and was later able to describe his dilemma to me turned out to be the beginning of a wedge in this unconscious empathy.

Betty had long ago completed a two-year nursing degree, then helped put her five children through college and her husband through graduate school. Then, at nearly sixty, she returned to finish her own undergraduate degree. Shortly afterward, she had to stop going to school for three months. She discovered that when she wasn't actively being a student "everybody just reverted right back to depending on me in ways that I didn't even realize they were . . . 'Mom could do this,' 'Betty can do that'. . . . It was just automatic, sort of. I was the one that recognized it and said, 'Hey,'" she laughed as she remembered, "'this is not gonna work for me'. . . . They'd all been so relieved that I wasn't in school that quarter and now I could—it could be like it was. Then they realized it's not ever going to be like it was. . . . After all," she chuckled again, "I have my life, too."

Yet Betty had once been much like Patrick. She had once unequivocally "been there" to care for others—her patients and her family—even at the cost of her own dreams and desires. Now, however, something had changed. In addition to her well-developed sense of empathy she had developed a new ability—to recognize it as a feeling and not necessarily as an imperative. Furthermore, Betty has come to see *herself* as among those for whom she has a right and even an obligation to care.

According to Kegan (1994), the capacity *both* to experience *and* to observe oneself experiencing is a hallmark of development beyond the position of being defined by others (third-order consciousness), toward the position of self-definition (fourth-order consciousness). Betty is able to examine her feelings in light of the situation and make choices. However, she can also choose to respond to others in ways they might deem selfish without feeling herself to be at the mercy of their assessment. Patrick, by comparison, cannot revisit his commitment to his neighbor in light of his new situation as a student. Although he provided his truck and his son, he empathizes with his neighbor's (imagined) disappointment (who, after all, might have been more than satisfied with the substitute services of a strapping, energetic teenager). Nor can he go next door, explain his new circumstances, and agree to give his friend an hour of his time, because then he would have failed *my* expectations of him! Patrick's third-order self is constructed by and through all of the ways he relates to others—a construction that he is unaware of, as he is "inside" it. Anyth. that challenges or puts these connections at risk also threatens the person he knows himself to be. Although he described his dilemma in nearly those exact words, he does not recognize this belief as his own construction and hence as open to change. To Patrick, it simply *is* who he is: an incontestable "reality."

Betty, however, has developed a more complex (fourth-order) self-construction that lets her be "outside," a position from which she can still empathize but also observe herself being empathetic (Taylor, 1995). She can acknowledge her feelings, yet she has a choice about whether to act on them. As a result, her definition of "self" as a loving, caring person does not depend on taking care of others no matter what the cost to her own desires and designs. She sees others "as responsible for [their] behaviors and herself as responsible for the feelings she has about those behaviors" (Kegan, 1994, p. 121). In Betty, then, we see many of the characteristics of this shift from third- to fourth-order consciousness.

Implications for Adult Education

One goal for adult educators should be encouraging just such new perspectives as Kegan describes. But what kind of learning might lead to a deepened understanding of oneself, one's responsibility, and one's capacity to act in the world?

Those addressing this question in terms of perspective transformation (Mezirow and Associates, 1990; Cranton, 1994) have devised multiple strategies to achieve these ends, such as metaphor analysis and educational biographies. Two colleagues and I (Taylor, Marienau, and Fiddler, forthcoming) have addressed these questions more broadly by exploring the literature of adult learning and adult development, reflecting on our own practice, and consulting adult educators on three continents. The results of our research first yielded a list of "developmental outcomes." These outcomes describe an evolving, growing learner who can (1) engage with the world of ideas and learn from experience, (2) examine and challenge assumptions, (3) arrive at commitments through self-reflection, and (4) relate to others from a place of mutual enhancement rather than need. When we then asked educators how they accomplished these goals, we discovered that what we had taken for outcomes were really intentions. For one thing, no one can develop anyone else; for another, as Daloz (1988) has pointed out, educators must also honor adults' decisions *not* to develop in these ways. Nevertheless, these intentions informed instructional design.

We found that teaching with developmental intentions usually begins with experiences that help to surface learners' existing ideas and beliefs. Learners then reflect, using some framework(s) of analysis to which they may also have contributed. Individually and as a group they then begin to construct new meaning. Such teaching and learning encourages "transformation of consciousness . . . toward self-authorship" and self-definition (Kegan, 1994, pp. 300–301). In addition, these processes foster thinking that is "inclusive, discriminating, and open to experiences [as well as open] to alternative perspectives . . . [rather than thinking that is] rigid and highly defended" (Mezirow, 1991, p. 156). As with Betty and Patrick, we begin to glimpse the possibilities inherent within the educational experience to shift consciousness and achieve a new understanding of the self and our relationship to the world.

References

Bee, H. L. *The Journey of Adulthood.* (3rd ed.) Upper Saddle River, N.J.: Prentice Hall, 1996.

Bergman, S. J., and Surrey, J. L. "The Woman-Man Relationship: Impasses and Possibilities." In J. V. Jordan (ed.), *Women's Growth in Diversity.* New York: Guilford Press, 1997.

Cranton, P. *Understanding and Promoting Transformative Learning.* San Francisco: Jossey-Bass, 1994.

Daloz, L. A. "The Story of Gladys Who Refused to Grow: A Morality Tale for Mentors." *Lifelong Learning,* 1988, *11* (4), 4–7.

Erikson, E. H. *Identity and the Life Cycle.* Psychological Issues Monograph 1. New York: International Universities Press, 1959.

Gilligan, C. *In a Different Voice: Psychological Theory and Women's Development.* Cambridge, Mass.: Harvard University Press, 1982.

Jordan, J. V., Kaplan, A. G., Miller, J. B., Stiver, I. P., and Surrey, J. L. *Women's Growth in Connection.* New York: Guilford Press, 1991.

Kegan, R. *The Evolving Self: Problem and Process in Human Development.* Cambridge, Mass.: Harvard University Press, 1982.

Kegan, R. *In over Our Heads: The Mental Demands of Modern Life.* Cambridge, Mass.: Harvard University Press, 1994.

Koller, A. *An Unknown Woman: A Journal of Self-Discovery,* 1981.

Mezirow, J. *Transformative Dimensions of Adult Learning.* San Francisco: Jossey-Bass, 1991.

Mezirow, J., and Associates. *Fostering Critical Reflection in Adulthood.* San Francisco: Jossey-Bass, 1990.

Miller, J. B. *Toward a New Psychology of Women.* Boston: Beacon Press, 1976.

Miller, J. B., and Stiver, I. P. *The Healing Connection.* Boston: Beacon Press, 1997.

Peck, T. A. "Women's Self-Definition: From a Different Model?" *Psychology of Women Quarterly,* 1986, *10,* 274–284.

Shafer, R. "Generative Empathy in the Treatment Situation." *Psychoanalytic Quarterly,* 1959, *28* (3), 342–373.

Taylor, K. "Sitting Beside Herself: Self-Assessment and Women's Adult Development." In K. Taylor and C. Marienau (eds.), *Learning Environments for Women's Adult Development: Bridges Toward Change.* New Directions in Adult and Continuing Education, no. 65. San Francisco: Jossey-Bass, 1995.

Taylor, K., Marienau, C., and Fiddler, M. *Developing Adult Learners: Strategies for Teachers and Trainers.* San Francisco: Jossey-Bass, forthcoming.

KATHLEEN TAYLOR *is chair of the Department of Portfolio Development, Saint Mary's College of California, Moraga.*

8

How adults change over time is best understood through a consideration of the intersection of historical time period, chronological age (life time), and the culturally specific social timetable that orders major life events.

Time as the Integrative Factor

Sharan B. Merriam

A developmental perspective on the life course is about documenting change over time, or change with the passage of time. Time, therefore, is a key variable in studying development and in understanding the nature if not the causes of change. But development is not simply a function of the ticking of the clock and the passage of years. Except for certain physiological changes such as the greying of hair or menopause, just getting older is too simple an explanation to account for changes in behavior, attitude, values, or self-perception. Intertwined with the mere passage of time is the historical context in which one lives as well as the social expectations of a particular culture at a particular point in time.

Time thus has three connotations when applied to development: (1) the passage of time marked by chronological age, (2) historical time, or the particular period in history in which one lives, and (3) social time—a culturally dependent timetable outlining appropriate behavior at various stages in the life cycle. As a multidimensional concept incorporating biological, sociocultural, and historical dimensions, time can indeed function as an integrative mechanism in the study of adult development. After reviewing the three kinds of time and their role in development, I will illustrate how time is an integrative concept with a study of HIV-positive men and women.

Three Kinds of Time

In studying and understanding adult development, time is among the most powerful of the multiple influences that might account for patterns of change over time. Neugarten (1976) and Baltes (1987) have each presented models of time—Baltes calls them influences—that are widely referenced in the literature and have helped to frame some research. These two models overlap; I discuss them together.

Historical Time. Both Neugarten and Baltes acknowledge the historical context as crucial to the understanding of development. Neugarten and Datan (1973, p. 58) define *historical time* as "long-term processes, such as industrialization and urbanization," and "economic, political, and social events that directly influence the life course of the individuals who experience those events." Baltes (1987) uses the term *history-graded influences* for the same phenomena.

Both models underscore the importance of the interaction between historical time and the chronological age of individuals or groups of individuals of approximately the same age or cohort. In other words, the nature of the impact of particular historical processes or events on development depends on the age or life stage of the individual at the time of the occurrence. This interaction is easily illustrated by the computer "revolution" of the current historical period. The ease with which most young people deal with computers versus the way older cohorts do has much to do with position in the life cycle; growing up with computers as part of everyday life is a very different scenario from learning to use one for the first time at age fifty.

Research in life span development also demonstrates this interaction. Schaie's (1994) studies of intelligence and aging suggest that intelligence changes with age and historical time; successively older cohorts have had fewer years of formal education, hence their average scores on tests are lower than younger cohorts, although there may be as much variance within one cohort as another. In addition to education accounting for some of the differences, improvements in health and medical care—also aspects of historical time—have likely affected successive cohorts.

Life Time. In addition to historical or history-graded time, there is age-graded time. Age-graded influences are strongly associated with chronological age "and are therefore fairly predictable in their temporal sequence" (Baltes 1987, p. 621). Baltes includes both "biological maturation and age-graded socialization events" (p. 621) in this category, whereas Neugarten (1976) separates age-graded time into "life time" and "social time."

Life time is simply the number of years one has lived since birth—the passage of time measured in days, months, and years. Fry (1985) reminds us that time itself is a culturally constructed concept and that in Western societies it is a linear, "nonrepetitive straight line, divisible into years, days, hours, minutes, stretching from past to future" and that "the life course as an irreversible journey of personal development and aging between birth and death is reflective of this linear metaphor" (p. 221). Life time or chronological age is probably most useful when used in reference to biological changes, especially for earlier stages in the life cycle, for while the sequence of biological change remains fairly predictable, the rate at which these changes take place varies with increasing age. As Troll (1982) notes, "Variance on almost any characteristic increases with every decade of life" (p. 9). She goes on to point out that more useful indexes of physical or biological aging might be either developmental age—"how far an individual is toward maturity or death"—or functional age—an assessment of "how far along in his or her life span any person is" based on specific physiological measurements (p. 9). Thinking of differences in terms of developmental age may involve more than just physiological measures as the term *maturity* implies. Certainly maturity is also a function of sociocultural definitions, as well as of internal psychological processes. Hence, one may feel mature or function at a certain level of maturity as defined by one's internal, psychological clock in conjunction with sociocultural factors.

Chronological age or life time seems to function best in the study of adult development as a proxy or imperfect index of any number of factors—"biological, psychological, social, and self-perceived changes" (Kimmel, 1990, p. 31). It is clear that age in and of itself does not cause changes to take place over time; rather "we should look behind 'age' to see the time-dependent and time-independent processes that cause development" (Kimmel, 1990, p. 31). Neugarten and Neugarten (1987) have even suggested that we might be moving into an "age-irrelevant" society in which chronological age will be less and less helpful in understanding changes that go on in individual lives. The life cycle is more fluid, with the boundaries between major periods of the life span and age links to biological processes becoming blurred. To know someone is forty years old, for example, tells us little else about that person—physically, socially, or psychologically.

Social Time. Development is also shaped by the third kind of time— *social time*. Indeed, many would argue that it is a more powerful and direct influence, at least in adulthood, than life time or historical time. Social time is the transformation of calendar time into periods of the life cycle during which certain behaviors are expected and certain rights, responsibilities, and statuses characterize individual behavior in that stage of life. In all cultures "there exists a socially prescribed timetable for the ordering of major life events: a time in the life-span when men and women are expected to marry, a time to raise children, a time to retire" (Neugarten, 1976, p. 16). Individuals grow up learning and internalizing the social norms and expectations of their social group—"adults carry around in their heads, whether or not they can easily verbalize it, a set of anticipations of the normal, expectable life cycle" (Neugarten, 1976, p. 18). Although the norms may change over time and there is variation in the actual experiencing of these events, the overall "normative pattern is adhered to, more or less consistently, by most persons within a given social group" (p. 16). This social "clock" becomes internalized to the extent that individuals assess whether they are "on-time" or "off-time" with regard to the occurrence of events in their lives. Marrying late, changing careers in midlife rather than rising to the top in one's previous career, death of a parent early in a child's life, and so on, are examples of off-timed events in North American culture.

The ordering of our lives by a socially structured timetable serves several functions, according to Hagestad (1996). It reduces uncertainty, giving us "a sense of direction . . . in everyday life, the yearly cycle, and the life course" (p. 210). It also enables us to prepare for what lies ahead; we learn what to anticipate and when it is likely to occur. Negotiating transitions and adapting to life events is easier when such changes are anticipated and planned. Part of what makes them easier is that there is social support from peers who are going through the same experience at the same time. Finally, Hagestad suggests that social time offers us a means of "marking and evaluating progress in the life course, because we have some sense of how our movement compares to timetables" (p. 210).

Social norms change over time. For example, not having children is a much more viable option today than it was a few decades ago, as is returning to school later in life or beginning a new career in midlife. Regardless of long-term shifts in expectations, however, research suggests that contemporary age norms do exert a powerful influence on people's thinking. In a review of some research on social roles, social relations, and social change, Elder (1995) concludes that "timing matters . . . and it does so because we are guided by expectable timetables based on social arrangements and practices, age norms, and age-graded beliefs" (p. 122).

In addition to history-graded and age-graded (including life time and social time) influences, other factors influence development. These factors tend more toward pointing out how variation in the life course can occur. For example, Baltes's (1987) framework also consists of nonnormative influences. "Their major characteristic," according to Baltes (1987), "is that their occurrence, patterning, and sequencing are not applicable to many individuals, nor are they clearly tied to a dimension of . . . time" (p. 621). These are unique events that occur in some people's lives but not most people's, nor do they depend on age or life stage. Being in a car accident, winning a lottery, enduring the death of your child, achieving fame and so on, are examples of nonnormative influences on a person's development. Schlossberg, Waters, and Goodman (1995) refer to these as *unanticipated* life events or transitions, which can have as dominant an effect on shaping a person as the more common, socially normed, and anticipated life events.

Certainly as powerful as time in understanding development are gender, race, socioeconomic class, ethnicity, sexual orientation, able-bodiedness, and so on—factors addressed in other chapters in this volume. Whichever variables are placed at center stage in the study of adult development, time is always the backdrop against which changes are assessed. Time itself, however, has rarely been studied as an integrative factor for understanding the process of development.

The Influence of Time in the Development of HIV-Positive Adults

To illustrate the power of time as an integrative concept in understanding development, I draw on research with HIV-positive adults that my colleagues and I conducted over a two-year period. We first interviewed ten

HIV-positive men and eight HIV-positive women between the ages of eighteen and fifty-seven in late 1995. Our primary question then was how they had made meaning of this diagnosis and how they had integrated this meaning into their lives (Courtenay, Merriam, and Reeves, 1998). Two years later, in 1997, we were able to interview fourteen of the original eighteen participants. Our primary question in this follow-up study was the extent to which transformations in perspective that we had uncovered in our first study had been sustained over time (see Courtenay, Merriam, Reeves, and Baumgartner, forthcoming). It was in this second set of interviews that we became aware of the convergence of historical, life, and social time in shaping the lives of these men and women.

The AIDS epidemic is, of course, an example of a historical event that has affected not only the lives of those infected but the whole of society as well. In the two years between our studies, recent advances in the treatment of AIDS—also a function of historical time—were seen to have had a dramatic effect on the participants. Most were on protease inhibitors(PIs), and all reported improved health.

Some of our participants indicated an awareness of the role historical context was playing in their lives. Twenty-eight-year-old Dawn, whose viral load went from 650,000 to undetectable in two months, commented that "we understand so much more about this disease in the last two years, two to three years, than we have in the whole seventeen years of the epidemic." She is cautiously optimistic, though, recognizing that "the drugs are not a cure . . . this is a very smart bug." Also commenting on the impact of PIs at this particular time in the course of the epidemic, Steve said,

> I started to hear firsthand from my friends how phenomenally well everyone was doing and just physically to see them change within weeks. It was amazing. It really kind of lifted this . . . this mantle of this automatic death sentence, which everybody had been shouldering for years, ever since the onset of this. So, uh, I think the protease inhibitors have just been a wonderful, wonderful shot in the arm to everyone because they give such hope.

The advent of PIs and better understanding of the AIDS virus *at this particular time* in the history of the epidemic have intersected with the lives of the participants in our study. They have lived two more years and have hopes of living more years than they had ever thought possible when we first interviewed them in 1995. Reflecting on the additional two years that they have lived, their comments further illuminate another dimension of time—life time.

Life time, or the number of years a person has lived, is closely associated with changes in the physical body. The cessation of physiological systems is the end of life time, or death. In 1995, our participants were present-oriented, carefully monitoring the deterioration of their bodies as they psychologically prepared for death. When we interviewed our participants two years later, they had not only actually *lived* two more years than expected, they were cautiously optimistic about living a normal life span. Life time, or chronological age and its links to the physical body, was again a meaningful concept in their lives and their development. They were thinking of the future, making plans, trying to figure out a role to play as a person living rather than dying with a disease. Steve captures the optimism but also the quandary of "this idea that people are going to live; all right, now what?. . . We may be around until we're eighty or ninety. And if that's the case, now what do we do?" Jamie talks about having lived life in two-year segments. "Now suddenly," he says, "things are different. And, I'm looking and I'm saying, 'I'm healthier now than I was when I started in this thing, what if I live to be forty or forty-five or fifty?. . . What if I have a normal life, a normal life expectancy, when I haven't been planning?'. . . I haven't planned for long-term stuff. And now, suddenly, it looks as though I may have to. So, I mean it's much easier to plan to die than it is to plan to live."

With life time no longer suspended, one's social "clock" begins ticking. Our participants were again considering how to map out their lives and whether they were "on-time" or "off-time" in some of their plans. They were trying to figure out how to fit back into a context of socially prescribed norms and values—a context that had seemed irrelevant when we first interviewed them in 1995. Dawn, for example, who had been HIV-positive for ten years, comments: "You know, I don't know what it is to be twenty-something and not acutely aware of my own mortality." She plans to "take some time and kind of define what I'm gonna do for the next ten or twenty years." Some of her concerns sound typical of the age-thirty transition, which she herself identifies as a marker event: "Turning thirty . . . now it's becoming a reality." Having children has also been "a huge issue" for Dawn, "not one that I have yet resolved to my satisfaction." Jamie echoes Dawn's concerns about the off-timing of events in his life: "There's a lot of things that I probably would've gone through at twenty-three, twenty-four, that I didn't because I thought I was gonna be dead. Now all of a sudden I'm thinking I might not be dead, so now I have to go back to twenty-three and twenty-four and start thinking that way again."

Participants in their forties expressed typical midlife concerns, worrying about work and career, family and retirement. John, who at fifty-nine is the oldest participant in our study, is busily planning for his retirement to Florida in another year, including purchasing a condo and building his medical support system. Now that these men and women feel they have a future, social time influences their planning, their behavior, and their self-perceptions.

In summary, the AIDS epidemic, itself an advent of historical time, has affected people differently depending on their age. The interaction of historical time and cohort becomes obvious when we consider that thousands have already died and that the greatest impact has been on young adults— 91 percent of those infected are between the ages of twenty and forty-nine years of age (Ahmed, 1992).

Our participants, however, were affected by another historical event— the discovery of PIs. Improved health and the lifting of what most believed to be a certain death sentence, along with the fact that participants had actually *lived* another two years, precipitated a reengagement with life time. Chronological age again became a viable concept. Birthdays were important occasions, especially milestone birthdays, and concern with physical aging became more normalized. This new consciousness of life time interacted with social time in that most were trying to figure out how to reengage with the "normal expectable life cycle" (Neugarten, 1976, p. 18). Work, school, family, buying a home, planning for retirement and so on, occupied their thoughts.

Time, Learning, and Development

Much can be gleaned from this research example about the integrative nature of time and its relationship to learning and development. The construct of time becomes a window through which we can better understand the changes these participants made in their behaviors, attitudes, values, and meaning making. And the partialing out of historical time, life time, and social time gives us an even clearer picture of this interaction. On a pragmatic level, participants spoke of the steep learning curve in dealing with the initial diagnosis and then learning to live with HIV and AIDS. Further, most had undergone dramatic changes in perspective (see Courtenay, Merriam, and Reeves, 1998). Two years later, with the advent of PIs, participants were engaged in learning to live as healthfully as possible; some were even anticipating a normal life expectancy. They were also learning how to structure their lives in conjunction with normative social expectations.

That learning is integrally related to development is well established in the adult learning literature (Merriam and Caffarella, 1999). Less visible is the role of time in most research on development and learning. However, a closer examination of some of the learning and development literature does point to the crucial role of time. Havighurst's (1972) concept of the teachable moment, for example, posits that the optimum time for learning is in conjunction with developmental tasks that arise at certain periods in a person's life. Learning about parenting, beginning a career, or adjusting to the death of a spouse are developmental tasks that occur at particular times in the life cycle and give rise to the teachable moment. This concept is similar to one of Knowles's (1980) assumptions underlying andragogy—that an adult's readiness to learn is closely tied to the developmental tasks and social roles of adult life.

Even transformational learning, as presented by Mezirow (1991), Daloz (1986), Kegan (1994), and others, is inherently time-bound. Transformational learning is about fundamental change in a person's perspective, worldview, or cognitive structure. The process occurs in response to a personal life event or societywide event, the *timing* of which makes it particularly meaningful, setting in motion the examination of one's present assumptions. In fact, the timing of developmental tasks or life events can explain why the same event may have a dramatic effect on one person, whereas another person remains seemingly unaffected.

Although individual differences and commonalities in the developmental patterns and learning of adults can be explained by any number of factors, all such patterns are "within the stream of age-graded, history-graded, and nonnormative influences" (Baltes, 1987, p. 621). Time thus provides the context in which to understand developmental processes. And recognizing how time functions as an integrative concept for the process of development offers us a richer understanding of both adult development and adult learning.

References

Ahmed, R. "Immunological Memory Against Viruses." *Seminars in Immunology,* 1992, *4* (2), 105–109.

Baltes, P. B. "Theoretical Propositions of Life-Span Developmental Psychology: On the Dynamics Between Growth and Decline." *Developmental Psychology,* 1987, *23* (5), 611–626.

Courtenay, B. C., Merriam, S. B., and Reeves, P. M. "The Centrality of Meaning Making in Transformational Learning: How HIV-Positive Adults Make Sense of Their Lives." *Adult Education Quarterly,* 1998, *48* (2), 63–82.

Courtenay, B. C., Merriam, S. B., Reeves, P. M., and Baumgartner, L. M. "Perspective Transformation over Time: A Two-Year Follow-Up Study of HIV-Positive Adults." *Adult Education Quarterly* (forthcoming).

Daloz, L. A. *Effective Teaching and Mentoring: Realizing the Transformational Power of Adult Learning Experiences.* San Francisco: Jossey-Bass, 1986.

Elder, G. H., Jr. "The Life Course Paradigm: Social Change and Individual Development." In P. Moen, G. H. Elder Jr., and K. Luschner (eds.), *Examining Lives in Context: Perspectives on the Ecology of Human Development.* Washington, D.C.: American Psychological Association, 1995.

Fry, C. L. "Culture, Behavior and Aging in the Comparative Perspective." In J. E. Birren and K. W. Schaie (eds.), *Handbook of the Psychology of Aging.* New York: Van Nostrand Reinhold Company, 1985.

Hagestad, G. O. "On-Time, Off-Time, Out of Time? Reflections on Continuity and Discontinuity from an Illness Process." In V. L. Bengtson (ed.), *Adulthood and Aging: Research on Continuities and Discontinuities.* New York: Springer, 1996.

Havinghurst, R. J. *Developmental Tasks and Education* (3rd ed.), New York: McKay, 1972.

Kegan, R. *In over Our Heads: The Mental Demands of Modern Life.* Cambridge, Mass.: Harvard University Press, 1994.

Kimmel, D. C. *Adulthood and Aging: An Interdisciplinary, Developmental View.* (2nd ed.) New York: Wiley, 1990.

Knowles, M. S. *The Modern Practice of Adult Education: From Pedagogy to Andragogy.* (2nd ed.) New York: Cambridge Books, 1980.

Merriam, S. B., and Caffarella, R. S. *Learning in Adulthood.* (2nd ed.) San Francisco: Jossey-Bass, 1999.

Mezirow, J. *Transformative Dimensions of Adult Learning.* San Francisco: Jossey-Bass, 1991.

Neugarten, B. L. "Adaptation and the Life Cycle." *The Counseling Psychologist,* 1976, *6* (1), 16–20.

Neugarten, B. L., and Datan, N. "Sociological Perspectives on the Life Cycle." In P. B. Baltes and K. W. Schaie (eds.), *Life-Span Developmental Psychology: Personality and Socialization.* New York: Academic Press, 1973.

Neugarten, B. L., and Neugarten, D. A. "The Changing Meanings of Age." *Psychology Today,* 1987, *21* (5), 29–33.

Schaie, K. W. "The Course of Adult Intellectual Development." *American Psychologist,* 1994, *49* (4), 304–313.

Schlossberg, N. K., Waters, E. B., and Goodman, J. *Counseling Adults in Transition.* (2nd ed.) New York: Springer, 1995.

Troll, L. E. *Continuations: Adult Development and Aging.* Pacific Grove, Calif.: Brooks/Cole, 1982.

SHARAN B. MERRIAM is professor of adult education at the University of Georgia, Athens.

9

Narrative offers a way of understanding development in terms of the storied nature of human experience. This chapter discusses the contextual, interpretive, retrospective, and temporal dimensions of narrative as applied to adult development.

Understanding Adult Development as Narrative

Marsha Rossiter

I hung up the telephone with a mixture of happiness and anxiety as the realization came to me that a chapter in my life was coming to a close. I had just finished reviewing the graduation application process with my adviser. Tears welled up in my eyes. Shocked at myself and slightly embarrassed, as the call had been made from work, I immediately sought to suppress my emotions. But my mind drifted backward in time, recollecting the memories of the vision that I had set out to make a reality some years ago. The entire experience that lay before me was completely unimaginable to me at that point. College was what I considered only a means to an end, a means of deliverance into the company of the elite. And here I was this day, an altogether different self, realizing how the desire for a degree and the experience of it had changed me, and how truly satisfied I was with the transformation.

So begins Anne's story of returning to college as an adult. It is a story of difficulty, delays, uncertainty; it is also a story of discovery and change. It is a story of human development. Although we could apply various developmental theories to Anne's experience, our purpose in this chapter is to explore a narrative orientation toward adult development. We can begin by noting that *narrative* in simplest terms has to do with stories. As a noun, *narrative* is commonly used as another term for *story*; as an adjective it refers to the storied nature of something, as in narrative poetry. Therefore, to use the term *narrative* in connection with development is to look at the storied nature of development and think of story as a metaphor for human life.

In this chapter I first discuss aspects of a narrative orientation to development and then outline four qualities of narrative—the contextual, interpretive,

New Directions for Adult and Continuing Education, no. 84, Winter 1999 © Jossey-Bass Publishers

retrospective, and temporal—that are central to an understanding of development as narrative. In the final section, I suggest implications of this narrative
orientation to development for our understanding of adult learning. Excerpts
from Anne's story will serve as a reference to one adult's experience.

A Narrative Orientation

"The stories we hear and the stories we tell shape the meaning and texture
of our lives at every stage and juncture" (Witherell and Noddings, 1991, p. 1).
A narrative understanding of adult development is grounded in the assumption that narrative is a primary structure through which human beings organize and make meaning of their experience (Polkinghorne, 1988; Bruner,
1990). Sarbin (1986) states the "narratory principle" that "human beings
think, perceive, imagine, and make moral choices according to narrative
structures" (p. 8). Meaning is constructed, understood, and expressed in
story form. Thus, stories and storytelling are pervasive in human experience, communication, and symbolic activity. If we listen to ourselves in
everyday communication—around the dinner table, from the pulpit, in the
therapist's office, in the classroom—we can hear ourselves in the act of
storytelling. Although our everyday stories may be partial or fragmentary,
the narrative structure of our meaning making is apparent.

When we understand that the process of human meaning making takes
a narrative form and that people understand the changes over the course of
their own lives narratively, we can appreciate the value of the narrative orientation to the study of development. It is an approach that attempts to
describe development from the inside as it is lived rather than from the outside as it is observed. The focus is on subjective meaning—how people
make sense of the events of their lives over the life course. Developmental
change is experienced through a constructed personal narrative that is
revised and enlarged over time to accommodate new insights, unanticipated
events, and transformed perspectives.

The assumptions and methods of narrative psychology are congruent
with those of human science. As Polkinghorne (1988) and others have
argued, the methods developed by physical sciences to study nonhuman
entities are not appropriate for the study of human beings. The natural science orientation emphasizes logical and deductive thought processes, the
study of discrete decontextualized parts of the whole, and knowledge for
the purposes of prediction and control.

In contrast, the narrative or human science orientation deals in the realm
of human meaning and experience. It emphasizes inductive processes, con-
textualized knowledge, and human intention; it aims toward description and
interpretation rather than explanation. The narrative approach to development is holistic in that it acknowledges the cognitive, affective, and motiva-
tional dimensions of meaning making. It also takes into account the biological
and environmental influences on development. The narrative approach may

provide a better understanding of the life course than the explanatory model of the natural sciences because it parallels the approach actually used by persons in their interpretations of their own lives (Cohler, 1982).

We can also compare the narrative orientation to adult development with the organismic model of development that is generally considered the framework for stage theories. The metaphor underlying the organismic model is, of course, the living organism. Just as a living organism grows physically from birth to maturity in a predictable pattern, psychological development is understood in terms of ordered change leading toward a given endpoint. This approach assumes a fixed sequence of stages or tasks in which each stage follows from the preceding one in invariant order. The narrative orientation to development is an expression of contextualism in which the historical event is the central metaphor. (See Sarbin, 1986, and Hermans, 1997, for a discussion of root metaphors and development.) As such, narrative attends to the context in which events occur, whether they are predictable or not. As Freeman (1991) observes, a good deal of human life has to do with responding to unanticipated happenings. Indeed, the construction of the personal narrative is seen as a means of maintaining coherence and unity during times of transition. Thus the life narrative, through which development is experienced and expressed, is not fixed but is told and retold in response to situational change throughout the life course.

In summary, a narrative orientation to adult development assumes that (1) narrative is a basic structure of human meaning making, (2) adult development is experienced and expressed through the construction of self stories, (3) a human science approach is appropriate for the study of adult development, and (4) adult development proceeds in ways that are not necessarily predictable. Narrative is not only a method for the study of lives but a construct that refers to the product of meaning making—the personal narrative.

Adult Development as Narrative

To appreciate development as narrative is to consider its storied nature. In this section I elaborate on the contextual, interpretive, retrospective, and temporal dimensions of story and narrative and discuss how each applies to an understanding of adult development.

Contextual. To think of development as story suggests the importance of the internal context, that is, the story's coherence and plot. A story, after all, is not simply an assortment or sequence of events; the events of a story are related to one another in some meaningful way. And the way in which the events relate to one another is determined by the relative valuation of possible outcomes. That is, events are understood according to whether they render a valued goal more or less attainable. Just as any character's action in a story can only be understood in reference to the plot of the story in which the character is acting, so it is with human development—events of one's life mean something in relation to other events and in relation to the valued ends toward which a person is striving.

Further, the narrative orientation is sensitive to the cultural milieu within which development takes place. The individual life narrative is not constructed in a vacuum but is situated in time and place, in society and family, in national, religious, and ethnic traditions—all of which form the basis of a shared sociocultural meaning system. Every person's life narrative is a personal rendition—selections, rejections, omissions—of the motifs of those larger narratives in which one's experience is situated. Development involves becoming aware of those narratives and their constraining or enriching influences on our lives.

Consider Anne's description of her decision to go to college a few years after high school:

> My parents had worked in factories most of their lives, and they were the kind of people who kept mostly to themselves. They struggled financially. . . . As a loan processor at the bank, part of my duties included maintaining student loan accounts. The names of former high school classmates passed across my desk, some of whom were entering their last year of college. These were people I had grown up with who were moving on with their lives, building for themselves the foundations for their future. Yet, where was I going? Who was I going to be in comparison to what these people were going to be? It finally dawned on me that no one was going to build a life for me that was separate and distinct from the life my parents had led, except me.

Anne frames the decision to go to college in relation to her parents—building a life that is different from theirs—and in relation to her former classmates. The going-to-college experience takes on significance *as a developmental event* for Anne that is quite different from the meaning it has for a person who goes to college as a result of parental expectation. Stories of development are highly individual, but at the same time they are expressions of larger cultural or familial narratives.

Interpretive. A story is not a collection of facts, a logical argument, or a scientific proposition; it is, rather, an account of events emplotted according to human values, intentions, and purposes. As such it calls for interpretation. When we read a story, the meaning we make of it is some mix of what is told in the story and what we bring to it from our own store of knowing. The story of development, then, is not simply an account of what happened or a prediction of what will happen. Instead, it involves the interpretation of events and behaviors; of course, multiple interpretations of the same event can exist.

In understanding development as narrative, the interpretation that is privileged is that of the person whose development is in question. As I mentioned, a narrative orientation is experience-based. Developmental theories offer particular interpretations of certain human behaviors, and those interpretations are oriented to the assumed or posited endpoint of development.

The narrative perspective, with its emphasis on context and experience, questions the universality of any such a priori ends. Development as narrative begins with the person's own assessment of progress toward her or his purposes and goals; the person's subjective valuation of events and changes is of primary importance. As Freeman (1991) points out, we can say that people develop when they change in ways that *they understand* as creating "a more comprehensive and inclusive interpretive context within which to place their experience" (p. 96).

Anne's statement of her own growth is an example of this self-interpretation. She writes:

> I am satisfied that the struggle to redefine my sense of self as separate from my parents has been accomplished. I have created a possible self from an imagined self. . . . I do not feel the constraints of 'keeping to myself' as my parents did, but have allowed the learning process to comfortably flow into other aspects of my life, perpetuating experimentation with new possibilities.

In this case, she has moved toward independence from her parents. That is a common developmental task of young adulthood, but more important from a narrative perspective is her valuation of it. This self-interpretation is not something determined once and finally—meanings are reinterpreted throughout the course of one's life. The life narrative at any given time reflects a person's current subjective interpretation of the meaning of events and experiences of her or his life (Cohler, 1982).

Retrospective. Narrative, in a sense, is history—the telling of what has gone before. Accordingly, to understand development as narrative is to take a backward-looking, retrospective stance. It does not project a predetermined telos toward which development inevitably is progressing, nor is it focused on identifying those patterns, events, or stages that will predict development. A narrative perspective attends to what can be understood about human development through its telling and retelling. Although the narrative perspective moves away from the idea of development as progress toward some predetermined endpoint or final stage, it does incorporate the idea of an internally created telos or "ideal" according to which development is assessed (Hermans, 1997).

Freeman (1991) has explicated the understanding of development as retrospective: "In a distinct sense development is a fundamentally retrospective concept, predicated on what has been here called rewriting the self: It is only after one has arrived at what is arguably or demonstrably a better psychological place than where one has been before that development can be said to have occurred" (p. 99).

Often the developmental significance of a decision or an event is not recognized until after the fact, as in the case of Anne's decision to join the National Guard as a means to help finance her college education. In looking back, she says:

How ludicrous it seems to me today that I marched off my job and into the Army without blinking an eye. But, I had proven to myself that I could be a student, and it was apparently not hard for me to picture myself as a soldier. And a soldier I became. How little credit I gave this decision as another transformative life experience. How little did I realize that this affiliation would change who I was.

Temporal. The idea of narrative includes—requires—a temporal dimension. Just as one still frame is not a movie, so one moment frozen in time is not a story. Narrative suggests movement, fluidity, and an unfolding of events through time. As an orientation to human development, narrative highlights this temporal flow in its attention to formation and re-formation over form, to processes over states of being, to meaning making over predetermined checkpoints along the life course. The implications of this temporality are subtle yet profound as we apply this notion to an understanding of adult development.

Narrative assumes a dynamic interrelationship between time and meaning. An understanding of past and future is continually evolving in the present. When we read a novel or watch a movie, we move through the story on a wave of understanding that joins our sense of what has already happened with our anticipation of what might come next. Similarly, we experience the course of life in reference to time; in existential terms, *human being* is *being-in-time*. The present moment, in which we are perpetually poised and from which we recollect the past and imagine the future, is everflowing. There is no plateau of development during which time stops so that we remain cast in a particular stage for a period of time; there is no external vantage point outside the flow of time from which to observe the end from the beginning. We are always within time. Thus, the individual construction of the life narrative, like time itself, is open-ended and ongoing; the "plot" is reworked and recast as time goes on, according to needs and perspective of the present self. We understand the meanings of the past, present, or future in relation to one another—as the present changes, so also does our interpretation of the past and our vision of a possible future.

Implications for Adult Learning

An appreciation of development as narrative enriches our understanding of adult learners and the place of learning in their lives. It does not replace but complements other perspectives and theories of development. As I have outlined, narrative development focuses on the *meaning* of changes and events over the life course; it therefore suggests implications for our understanding of learning that have to do with meaning making and transformation.

Following are four statements that derive from an understanding of adult development as narrative; the commentary points to the implications of each for adult educators.

1. *Learners are experts on their own development.* Because the narrative perspective attempts to understand development as it is lived, it views adults as valuable sources of information about their own development. Attention to their subjective interpretation of where they are in life, where they are going, and how well they are progressing toward their chosen ends is essential to an understanding of their development—and their learning. As adult educators, we bring to the teaching-learning encounter an array of developmental theories and perspectives that outline stages and phases of adulthood. This is valuable knowledge for the adult educator, but according to the narrative view it is partial; the "rest of the story" of learners' development can—and must—be told by learners themselves. This stance calls into question an implicit assumption about who is the expert on learners' development. As long as we as educators hold the knowledge of development, we hold the power to define what constitutes "progress" and "growth." Acknowledging the validity of the learners' definition of their own developmental path is an empowering and respectful teaching orientation—and it yields fuller understanding of developmental change.

2. *Narratives mediate change.* As adult educators, we frequently encounter learners at a time of transition in their lives; indeed it is the link between learning and change that inclines us in the direction of understanding developmental processes. Change—whether brought about through an intentional transition, "normative" development, or an unexpected event in life—presents new circumstances and evidence that cannot be ignored in one's personal meaning system. The resulting conflicts, contradictions, and disorienting dilemmas may stimulate learning.

In this regard, the contribution of the narrative perspective is its appreciation of the fact that change stimulates the storying process. Bruner (1990) speaks of storying as a means to deal with the noncanonical in both individual and cultural meaning systems. When something happens that is outside the canon of our habitual patterns of thought and belief, we tell stories about it to tame it, so to speak, and to understand it. We revise meanings in such a way as to accommodate the out-of-the-ordinary, the new ideas or conflicting beliefs. Because narrative is, experientially, the form that meaning takes, the re-formation of meaning is a matter of re-storying. The point is that the act of learning—particularly at a time of transition in life—will stimulate the narrative impulse. Learners will create new stories to assimilate new ideas into their own meaning systems.

3. *The telling of the life narrative leads development.* As we have seen, the narrative orientation attends to an adult's subjective assessment of her or his own development. This self review of the life story actually furthers development. The act of telling one's story externalizes it so that one becomes more aware of the themes and topics that dominate one's life. Once that awareness takes place, a person can question whether or not to continue along the same lines (Hermans, 1997). The point is that the very act of telling or writing the story of one's own development enables a person to

step back from it, to reflect on it, and to make choices about how to interpret it and how to change it. This—making choices about one's life narrative—is the key to understanding the power of telling one's story. To be the teller or author of a story is to have authority over it—to choose what to tell and how to tell it, to determine the kind of story that it will be. This connection between authority and authorship makes the telling of the self-narrative empowering and potentially transformative.

4. *Adults re-story their lives in the process of transformative learning.* Mezirow's (1991) transformation theory has dominated the dialogue related to transformative learning in the literature of adult education. Mezirow has said that a "strong case can be made for calling perspective transformation the central process of adult development" (p. 155). A narrative orientation makes a case for understanding *re-storying* as the central process of development; certainly it suggests that which is transformed is not necessarily— or not only—a meaning perspective but rather the life narrative. Randall's (1996) idea of a three-stage process of transformative learning as "re-storying" the self parallels, in certain respects, Mezirow's process of perspective transformation; it (1) moves from a narrower to a more inclusive perspective, (2) involves recognizing the limitations of one's existing meaning system, (3) requires critical reflection on one's situation and options, and (4) culminates in action according to a changed way of being in the world.

In fact, we might say that the re-storying process tells the story of perspective transformation. We can say too that self-narration is a process more inclusive of the affective, spiritual, symbolic, and experiential dimensions of learning and change than perspective transformation as described by Mezirow. What distinguishes the re-storying process from perspective transformation is its subjective and interpretive nature. Transformation theory emphasizes rational discourse as a means through which meaning perspectives are validated consensually. In the re-storying process, there is no such striving for rationality and objectivity. The story of personal transformation is assessed according to the criteria for a good story—coherence, followability, verisimilitude.

Conclusion

This chapter has outlined a narrative orientation to adult development based on the fundamental assumption that narrative is a central structure of human meaning. Such an orientation is experience-based, holistic, and in accord with the methods of human science. The storied nature of adult development is understood in terms of the contextual, interpretive, retrospective, and temporal dimensions of narrative. It is through the ongoing construction of the self-narrative that developmental change is experienced and understood.

Anne's final comments on the completion of her degree capture the open-ended and constructive nature of development as narrative. She concludes:

I am not of the elite I once imagined that I would be upon degree completion. Instead, I know that my knowledge is only a fraction of what there is to know and that knowing is a lifelong learning experience. I will not be the same self a decade from now that I am today, but I am conscious of that self and have goals for a new self.

References

Bruner, J. *Acts of Meaning.* Cambridge, Mass.: Harvard University Press, 1990.

Cohler, B. J. "Personal Narrative and the Life Course." In P. B. Baltes and O. G. Brim Jr. (eds.), *Life-Span Development and Behavior.* New York: Academic Press, 1982.

Freeman, M. "Rewriting the Self: Development as Moral Practice." In M. B. Tappan and M. J. Packer (eds.), *Narrative and Storytelling: Implications for Understanding Moral Development.* New Directions for Child Development, no. 54. San Francisco: Jossey-Bass, 1991.

Hermans, H.J.M. "Self-Narrative in the Life Course: A Contextual Approach." In M. Bamberg (ed.), *Narrative Development: Six Approaches.* Mahwah, N.J.: Erlbaum, 1997.

Mezirow, J. *Transformative Dimensions of Adult Learning.* San Francisco: Jossey-Bass, 1991.

Polkinghorne, D. E. *Narrative Knowing and the Human Sciences.* Albany, N.Y.: State University of New York, 1988.

Randall, W. L. "Restorying a Life: Adult Education and Transformative Learning." In J. E. Birren, G. M. Kenyon, J. E. Ruth, J.J.F. Schroots, and T. Svensson, (eds.), *Aging and Biography: Explorations in Adult Development.* New York: Springer, 1996.

Sarbin, T. "The Narrative as a Root Metaphor for Psychology." In T. R. Sarbin (ed.), *Narrative Psychology: The Storied Nature of Human Conduct.* New York: Praeger, 1986.

Witherell, C., and Noddings, N. *Stories Lives Tell: Narrative and Dialogue in Education.* New York: Teachers College Press, 1991.

MARSHA ROSSITER is associate director of the Division of Continuing Education and Extension at the University of Wisconsin, Oshkosh.

10

Spirituality is a central aspect of human life. This chapter examines the process of spiritual development and how it is informed by culture.

The Spiritual Dimension of Adult Development

Elizabeth J. Tisdell

Scene 1: I was sitting in a church pew at the Unity Temple in Oak Park, Illinois, where I had recently moved from Seattle. Frank Lloyd Wright, a native of Oak Park, had built this temple in 1909. I was wondering about the stirrings in his own soul that prompted this famous architect to develop his particularly unique, angular architectural style that has become such an icon of American culture. A few minutes later, the minister began her sermon with the question, What is spirituality?—a question that human beings have pondered since the beginning of time. My eyes were drawn to the corners of this dwelling—to Frank Lloyd Wright's "angles of connection" that literally hold this temple together.

A week later, I was at my mother's bedside at the hospital.

Scene 2: At seventy-seven, with failing body, my mother still has a sharp, ageless mind that makes her a fascinating conversationalist, yet sometimes she is sharp and pointed in her critique of her own and others' lives. In reviewing her life, she often tells touching, tender, or funny stories of her own parents and grandparents, her five children, or of my father (her husband of fifty-four years). Sometimes she talks of her ambivalence toward the Catholic Church of her Irish American culture, for my mother, while always a faithful attendee at Sunday mass, found her own way of being a seeker of truth. As a science teacher and as one committed to keen analysis, she was never willing to give up her own good mind to popes or anyone else.

But on this Sunday, in failing health, she told only a couple of stories; mostly she wanted to be touched, to be held, to feel the warmth of human connectedness. And I, a middle-aged daughter of forty-three, was grateful that I could be present and connected in this physical contact that transcended a mother's and daughter's power struggles, or my own irritations about her negative comments on the length of my hair.

Scene 3: Just a couple of days ago, I was talking to an adult educator about her own thoughts on spirituality and how it affects her practice in teaching in a community college setting. Toward the end of our conversation she reflected on her own spirituality in relationship to being an African American woman and her involvement in social justice efforts: "I think all people have a spiritual part to them. For me it's the main part. I believe that there is a higher power that keeps the universe in balance. It's like the intellect—it's not as muscular in some people as it is in others, but it's there in everyone, whether they know it or not. I think my responsibility is great because I know what people went through so that I could have the freedom and the power to move forward in the world, so I must get up! And I must dig deep! And I must do good! And to not do that would be an affront to my ancestors, who stayed alive, and stayed strong, and stayed spiritually connected through centuries of brutality and everything, beyond slavery. That's what it is for me."

I began this discussion of the spiritual dimension of adult development with three recent scenes from my own life for a couple of reasons. First, *spirituality* is an elusive term; it is difficult to define and can be defined more easily through examples. These three scenes are ordinary; most of us could describe similar scenes. Yet they are extraordinary, at least to me. They helped me come to new insight, to a renewed sense of history and human connectedness, a new sense of meaning. Perhaps this gets at something of the essence of spirituality—discovering the extraordinary in the ordinary business of life.

But I also use the scenes as an entry point to this discussion because they hint at something more about the *possible manifestations* of spirituality in people's lives. All three vignettes suggest that spirituality highlights a sense of the connectedness of history, as well as the interconnectedness and unity of life and a sense of transcendence through what many define as a higher power. The first vignette also suggests what Wuthnow (1998), in his study of spirituality in America since the 1950s, refers to as "a spirituality of dwelling"—a spirituality that is tied to a sense of place or to a religious tradition. It also gets at a sense of creativity; Frank Lloyd Wright's creativity spanned the country and contributed to a "spirituality of dwelling" for many.

The second vignette focuses more on a sense of connectedness through the interweaving of our lives in long-term relationships with loved ones past and present through a legacy of storytelling and of loving relationships that transcend power struggles and human weakness. It also gets at what Wuthnow (1998) refers to as a "spirituality of seeking"—a spirituality that moves beyond dwelling places and religious traditions to ways of seeking truth while wandering through the journey of life, much the way my mother has done.

Finally, in the third vignette there is not only a sense of history and human connectedness but a sense of a spirituality of moral responsibility to carry on the work for justice of ancestors and others who forged ahead to create a better world in the face of adversity. And it points out that people's experience of spirituality is also embedded in a particular sociocultural history. Indeed, these three manifestations of spirituality—dwelling, seeking, and acting in the name of justice—are not the only manifestations of spirituality, but they are ways of beginning to frame our discussion here.

With the exception of the subfield of adult religious education, spiritual development has been given little attention in mainstream academic adult education. As Wuthnow (1998) observes, "Some proclaim that the dry spell of secularism is over; others wonder whether 'spiritual' has become synonymous with 'flaky'" (p. 1). Perhaps academics are wary of being associated with it. Or perhaps it's because *spirituality* is difficult to define. Yet, more recently the language of spirituality has begun to creep into some adult education discussions. Hart and Holton (1993) suggest that it offers hope to emancipatory education efforts, and Dirkx (1997) notes that attention to the soul in adult learning is important, particularly in attending to group process.

My discussion of these issues is in three parts. Because most discussions of spirituality are framed from a psychological perspective, I begin with that. Next, I look at some of the ways that culture informs spiritual development. Finally, I discuss the implications for adult education practice.

Psychological Perspectives on Spiritual Development

Most discussions of spiritual development are framed exclusively from a psychological perspective that focuses on the spiritual or faith development of the individual. Best known is the work of James Fowler (1981), who outlines a stage model of faith development. He defines *faith* as "not always religious in its content or context. . . . It is our way of finding coherence in and giving meaning to the multiple forces and relations that make up our lives" (p. 4). Fowler uses the term *faith* the way others might use the term *spirituality*, as that which is connected to meaning making and, often, to a sense of the transcendent. Although he doesn't equate faith with a religious tradition, he based his theory of faith development on a sample of 359 people, 97 percent of whom were not only white but identified with the Judeo-Christian faith. So although Fowler in theory offers a broader and more inclusive definition of faith as related to meaning making and as *beyond* religious tradition, in fact his stage theory is based on a sample whose faith is deeply informed by a specific religious tradition—a white, Judeo-Christian tradition. He appears to be making some unstated assumptions about universality based on a limited cultural sample, yet he still offers some important insights about spiritual development that are particularly related to adult learning.

Fowler (1981) describes a six-stage process of faith development, drawing on Kohlberg's and Piaget's theories of moral and cognitive development. Yet he takes issue with them for "their restrictive understanding of the role of imagination in knowing, their neglect of symbolic processes generally and the related lack of attention to unconscious structuring processes other than those constituting reasoning" (p. 103).

The first two stages—intuitive-projective faith and mythic-literal faith—are experienced in childhood. Fowler suggests that most adults fall into one of the next three stages: Stage 3 (conventional faith) is a "conformist" stage; Stage 4 (individuative-reflective faith) is more critically reflective, individuated, and less prone to accept outside answers; and Stage 5 (conjunctive faith) is, in addition to being critically reflective, tuned into the power of symbols and images as a form of knowledge. Only one person in his sample was described as being in Stage 6 (universalizing faith).

Courtenay (1994) notes some limitations of Fowler and other stage theorists' work: their undefined last stage, their tendency to create hierarchical stages of development that privilege autonomy over connection and relationship, and their masculinist orientation (the model is a better overall fit for men than for women). In discussing the role of image and symbol in knowledge construction and in development, he writes:

> This forming of an image does not wait or depend upon conscious processes. The image unites "information" and feeling; it holds together orientation and affectional significance. As such, images are prior to and deeper than concepts. When we are asked what we think or know about something or someone, we call up our images, setting in motion a kind of scanning interrogation or questioning of them. Then in a process that involves both a forming and an expression, we narrate what our images "know" [p. 26].

Fowler provides data to illustrate the ways that knowing manifested through access to image and symbol is tied to both the faith-spiritual dimension and to critical reflection in those who were in Stage 5 and Stage 6. This is not a blind knowing but one that touches human beings at very deep levels. Some manifest such knowing through conscious articulation skills in conceptualizing and others through creative expression in story, art, poetry, music, and other forms of creative living, including social activism. But what Fowler ignores is the fact that these forms of knowing are also deeply connected to one's cultural background and the sociocultural context, an aspect I discuss next.

Spirituality in the Context of Culture

The sociocultural context has often been overlooked by developmental theorists—an oversight that inadvertently propagates a view of development based on the dominant culture: white, Judeo-Christian, and middle class. This is why Merriam and Caffarella (1999) are calling for more integrative perspectives that attend to how biological, social, and cultural factors such as race, gender, and sexual orientation affect development and learning. Given the role of image and symbol (both are often culturally bound) in the construction of knowledge, it is particularly important to consider how culture informs spiritual development. A number of writers from specific cultural groups discuss how image and symbol from within their culture inform spiritual knowledge construction, ways of living in community, and working for justice in the world. Although these writers are not discussing spiritual development directly, there are possible developmental implications to what they have written.

A healthy spirituality is both life affirming and affirming of one's identity. Chicana feminist Ana Castillo (1996) discusses how many Latinas have developed a culturally grounded and woman-positive spirituality that affirms their identity; Catholicism and all its symbols are deeply embedded in Mexican American culture. She also notes that for Latinas to embrace their cultural identity, they must on some level embrace the Catholic aspect of the culture. Yet Catholicism, and indeed many aspects of Latino culture, are deeply patriarchal, which presents a dilemma for Chicana feminists.

In looking at the meanings associated with Our Lady of Guadalupe in Mexican culture, Castillo examines the relationship of the Aztec goddess traditions with our Lady of Guadalupe. She suggests that for many Chicanas, the symbol of *La Virgen* is not the passive virgin as the Blessed Mother is portrayed in many ethnic-Catholic cultures but is re-framed as an activist liberator. Anzaldua (1987) also speaks to this point:

> Today, *La Virgen de Guadalupe* is the single most potent religious, political, and cultural image of the Chicano/mexicano. She, like my race, is a synthesis of the old world and the new, of the religion and culture of the two races in our psyche, the conquerors and the conquered. She is the symbol of the mestizo true to his or her Indian values. *La cultura chicana* identifies with the mother (Indian) rather than with the father (Spanish). . . . She is our spiritual, political and psychological symbol [p. 30].

Thus, in framing *La Virgen* as the Aztec/mother/goddess, the two-in-one-culture liberator, many Chicana feminists are able to create a meaningful and life-enhancing, woman-positive spirituality. Asian American writer Naomi Southard (1996) makes a similar point in discussing the role that the image and symbol, Kuan Yin—the feminine wisdom figure and Buddhist symbol of compassion—has played for Asian American women of both Christian and Buddhist background.

Spirituality is about constructing knowledge through image and symbol. But it is also about attempting to live or act in the world in accordance with one's spiritual path, which for many has an orientation to community.

Paula Gunn Allen (1992) speaks to the connection between culture, spiritual symbol, and the "personal choice–community responsibility" dialectic in American Indian communities. She notes:

> It is an ineradicable orientation toward a spirit-informed view of the universe. . . . This view is not merely private, for it is shared by all the members of tribal psychic reality. It is not exactly personal. . . . It is however subjective, for . . . all matters of the nonmaterial realms of being must be experienced within the subjective mind of each individual at least as much as within the particular part of the tribal gestalt that is activated by ceremony, ritual, and vision [p. 165].

Allen is suggesting that in American Indian communities, knowledge is constructed through ritual, symbol, and ceremony but is constructed by individuals in a cultural community for the development both of the individual and that community. It connotes ways of living in the world and working for justice in a holistic way that honors the earth and the creatures and people in it (Deloria, 1992). Such holistic life practices or ways of living based on one's spirituality can take many forms—perhaps in dietary habits, music, meditation practices, emphasis on mindfulness, particular ways of working for justice in the world, and ways of accessing inspiration to do so. But such practices cannot be torn from their cultural background; they inform all aspects of our lives.

For many, spirituality is a grounding place for working for justice in the world. This was particularly obvious in the civil rights movement and continues to be true today for many within the African American community. Patricia Hill Collins (1998) discusses the important interconnecting role that spirituality plays in black women's ways of knowing, including their intellectual tradition. She writes:

> Spirituality, especially that organized through and sanctioned by Black Christian churches, provides an important way that many African-American women are moved to struggle for justice. Defined as a collective expression of deep feeling that occurs within an overarching moral framework, spirituality remains deeply intertwined with justice in Black women's intellectual history. Spirituality moves many Black women and thus influences Black women's critical social theory in particularly ways [p. 244].

Collins suggests that for most black women intellectuals, their ways of knowing and their ways of working for justice must be understood within their spiritual tradition and their culture. Nor can this be separated from the struggle against racism.

These are some examples of how members of these cultural groups draw on the spiritual symbols and traditions of their own cultures to affirm their cultural and gender identity and to guide their moral action in the world. This suggests what I would consider, in many cases, an evolved spiritual develop-ment. It is unclear how Fowler might classify such approaches to spirituality in his stages of faith. But if, as Fowler suggests, spirituality is our way of giv-ing coherence and meaning to the multiple realities of our lives, then we must also take into account the power relations and systems of privilege and oppression that inform our lives. To ignore this in theories of adult develop-ment is to continue to privilege a particular cultural view of spiritual devel-opment.

Implications for Adult Education

So what are the implications here for adult educators working with adult learners? As Wuthnow (1998) observes, there is a renewed interest in spiri-tuality in America. But this genre of spirituality more often takes the shape of a spirituality of seeking that is more mobile and takes into account greater interaction with people who are of different cultural and religious traditions. So first, adult educators might want to note that a search for or an acknowl-edgment of the spiritual in the lives of adult learners is connected to the search for meaning that give our lives coherence. For all adults, this is con-nected to how we create meaning in our relationships with others. It is in our living and loving, in our attempts to move beyond power struggles in per-sonal relationships. It is in the stories we tell to stay connected to those we love. It is in the creativity of artists, as well as in the adult learner sitting by the classroom door. It is in how we struggle for justice, on behalf of ourselves and others, and in the spirituality of our ancestors that inspires us to work against racism and move forward in the world. And for many adults it is con-nected with how we understand a higher power or a transcendent being.

Second, in attending to spiritual development, adult educators need to recognize that adult learners bring all of this with them into the learning environment. Dirkx (1997) suggests that our interest in promoting adult learning is not so much to teach soulwork, or spirituality. It is to *nurture* soul, that is, "to recognize what is already inherent within our relationships and experiences, to acknowledge its presence with the teaching and learn-ing environment, to respect its sacred message" (p. 83). In considering how this plays out with grassroots emancipatory adult educators working with women in an international context, Walters and Manicom (1996) note that "spirituality is another aspect of 'where women are' as they seek to make sense of the world. . . . [I]t is a theme that is increasingly significant in pop-ular education practice as culturally distinct groups, women recovering 'womanist' traditions and ethnic collectives, draw on cultural and spiritual symbols in healing and transformative education" (p. 13).

Third, spirituality is about how people construct knowledge through images and symbols, which often emanate from the deepest core of our being and can be accessed and manifested through art, music, or other creative work. They often inspire how we act in the world in advocating for ourselves, or in working for justice on behalf of others. Adult educators who encourage adult learners to work with image and symbol and to critically reflect on the meanings and power such images hold, as Dirkx (1997) suggests, may be encouraging and facilitating spiritual development as adult learners continue to negotiate new knowledge and new meaning in the world.

Fourth, spiritual development and the meaning attached to image and symbol cannot be separated from the sociocultural context of the learner. Our identity is constantly shifting, and our understanding of culture and spirituality is always being renegotiated as we interact with others who are of different cultural and spiritual backgrounds. To fail to examine the cultural embeddedness of image and symbol and its connection to the past histories of learners or to their present lives and emerging futures is to inadvertently privilege a white, middle-class, Judeo-Christian understanding of development. If spirituality is, in part, what gives coherence to life, it is important to understand its cultural and symbolic value and its way of guiding action in the world to people of differing cultural backgrounds. For example, it is the cultural history of the African American community college educator cited at this chapter's opening that helps us understand why her spirituality continually requires that she work for justice in the world. Indeed, it is this connection to her past and present that motivates her action on behalf of justice. Obviously, this is not without cultural significance.

Finally, the connection of spirituality as the grounding place for the work of many emancipatory adult educators cannot be overlooked. Almost all adult educators writing on emancipatory education cite the important influence of Paulo Freire on their own work, yet few discuss the fact that Freire was a deeply spiritual man, strongly influenced by liberation theology (Freire, 1997). bell hooks (1994) also discusses the importance of spirituality in guiding her own educational practice for social change. If one thinks of education and work for social justice as an aspect of spiritual development, it may be that attention to spirituality can offer new insight to the connection between individual and social transformation.

Spirituality is an elusive concept. Perhaps this is so because it is all-encompassing and cannot be torn from other aspects of adult development. For many, *spirituality* is a term that connotes wholeness and that gives coherence to life. It informs our knowing in ways that are beyond our conscious awareness. Even though it is difficult to discuss what is both so elusive and so encompassing, this chapter is one attempt to begin the dialogue of what spiritual development might mean and its relationship to adult learning in the field of adult education. I look forward to continuing the dialogue.

References

Anzaldua, G. *Borderlands/La Frontera: The New Mestiza.* San Francisco: Aunt Lute, 1987.
Castillo, A. *Massacre of the Dreamers: Essays on Xicanisma.* Albuquerque: University of New Mexico Press, 1996.

Courtenay, B. "Are Psychological Models of Adult Development Still Important for the Practice of Adult Education?" *Adult Education Quarterly,* 1994, *44* (3), 145–153.

Deloria, V. *God Is Red.* Golden, Colo.: North American Press, 1992.

Dirkx, J. "Nurturing Soul in Adult Learning." In P. Cranton (ed.), *Transformative Learning in Action: Insights from Practice.* New Directions for Adult and Continuing Education, no. 74. San Francisco: Jossey-Bass, 1997.

Fowler, J. *Stages of Faith: The Psychology of Human Development and the Quest for Meaning.* San Francisco: HarperCollins, 1981.

Freire, P. *Letters to Christina.* New York: Routledge, 1997.

Gunn Allen, P. *The Sacred Hoop: Recovering the Feminine in American Indian Traditions.* Boston: Beacon Press, 1992.

Hart, M., and Holton, D. "Beyond God the Father and Mother: Adult Education and Spirituality." In P. Jarvis and N. Walters (eds.), *Adult Education and Theological Interpretations* (pp. 237–258). Malabar, Fla.: Krieger, 1993.

Hill Collins, P. *Fighting Words: Black Women and the Search for Justice.* Minneapolis: University of Minnesota Press, 1998.

hooks, b. *Teaching to Transgress.* New York: Routledge, 1994.

Merriam, S., and Caffarella, R. *Learning in Adulthood.* San Francisco: Jossey-Bass, 1999.

Southard, N. "Recovery and Rediscovered Images: Spiritual Resources for Asian American Women." In U. King (ed.), *Feminist Theology from the Third World.* New York: Maryknoll, 1996.

Walters, S., and Manicom, L. (eds.). *Gender in Popular Education.* London: Zed Press, 1996.

Wuthnow, R. *After Heaven: Spirituality in America Since the 1950s.* Berkeley, Calif.: University of California Press, 1998.

ELIZABETH J. TISDELL is associate professor of adult education at National Louis University in Chicago.

11

This chapter draws on information from previous chapters to assess where are with our thinking about adult development and to suggest linkages between this theory and learning in adulthood.

Development and Learning: Themes and Conclusions

Rosemary S. Caffarella, M. Carolyn Clark

The adult developmental literature has had, and continues to have, an enormous impact on the ways in which we conceptualize adult learning and on our practice as adult educators. For example, many adult educators adopt, as part of their practice, the goal of helping learners to be more self-directed in their learning. This goal has been fostered by numerous adult educators, but its major origins can be traced back to one of the five assumptions of andragogy: "as a person matures, his or her self-concept moves from that of a dependent personality toward one of a self-directing human being" (Knowles, 1980, p. 44). This tenet was grounded in the work of scholars from the psychological tradition of development who for years posited autonomy as the pinnacle of human development (for example, Maslow, 1970; Kohlberg, 1973).

Although autonomy has been challenged as the highest form of development by many researchers during the last two decades (for example, Gilligan, 1982; Caffarella and Olson, 1994), many adult educators still practice their craft as if being autonomous characterizes mature adult life. In other words, some developmental theory even drives research and practice in adult education long after that theory has been questioned and alternative theories proposed. Because the theories of adult development significantly affect adult education theory and practice, we need to ensure that our knowledge of these theories is current and that we understand how it can inform our practice.

In this chapter we first assess the initial framework we used in organizing this volume. We then discuss how our own thinking about developmental theory has changed, focusing specifically on how we define integrative models and the promise that approach offers for theorizing adult development. We conclude the chapter with an exploration of how thinking differently about adult development influences the ways in which we think about adult learning.

Revisiting the Typology of Adult Development

In Chapter One, we provided an introduction to the many facets of adult development and the links between development and learning. Our initial premise was that a four-component framework offered by Merriam and Caffarella (1999) would provide a useful starting point for thinking about different ways of understanding development in adulthood. Viewing development through biological, psychological, sociocultural, and integrative lenses allowed us and the other contributors to this volume to address both the complexities of development and how this knowledge can enrich our practice as adult educators.

We believe our initial sense has been borne out. This typology did give us a more complex and nuanced sense of the adult development process. But it also enabled us to see something else. When we consider the latest work in this area, across all four categories of our typology, we notice that we seem to be beyond (at least for now) the crafting of grand theories of development like those offered by Erikson (1982) or Levinson (1986). With the exception of the integrated models (which, as we noted in Chapter One are not yet well developed), more recent work seems to focus on specific dimensions of development and often on a combination of dimensions. This is true even in the traditional areas of biological and psychological development. As Mott observes, the physical aging process involves much more than just bodily changes; it includes both how we and others think about aging. Therefore, how we age becomes a function of a complexity of factors, including the connections among the mind, body, and the culture in which we live. Likewise Reeves, in her chapter on psychological development, notes that there have been numerous challenges to the explanatory powers of the more classical theories, among them the idea that autonomy is the hallmark of development and that contextual factors have relatively little influence on how adults develop. Now it is commonly accepted that connectedness and interdependence are as important in the developmental process as autonomy and that context is highly salient.

If the traditional approaches are waning, it is obvious that the newer perspectives are in full flower. The sociocultural frame, which emphasizes the social and cultural aspects of our lives as the primary forces that drive development, has received more attention in the developmental literature recently. In no small part this expanded attention is due to the increased saliency today of issues related to gender, race and ethnicity, and sexual identity. In her chapter Ross-Gordon presents multiple ways of understanding gender identity development and explores the extensive and complex impact of cultural forces on this process. Chávez and Guido-DiBrito introduce us to the work on racial and ethnic development—a body of literature that is of increasing importance as we struggle to embrace diversity in our society. And Edwards and Brooks, in their chapter on sexual identity development, explore the tensions between the essentialist and social constructionist perspectives on sexual orientation. Here again we see new work unfolding as nondominant modes of sexuality become more common and more socially accepted.

There has been a shift in the literature on adult development toward thinking about development in a more integrative way; we believe that the most significant and promising work is now being done in this frame. This trend toward integration and multiplicity of thought is two-dimensional. First, many scholars, even within the biological and psychological frames, are acknowledging the importance of taking into account elements from at least one other frame and often more than one, therefore arguing for a more holistic view of development. This trend was seen in all of the chapters we have summarized thus far. The second dimension relates to alternative ways of thinking about how development unfolds in adulthood. The four chapters in our section on integrative models illustrate this. Each provides a different lens through which to view the developmental process, and each produces a different picture. Taylor, in looking at the notions of separation and connection, points to the work of theorists who argue for a complex and changing balance between these fundamental drives. Merriam shows us how the various conceptualizations of time provide a new way of understanding change and development. Rossiter, in her discussion of development as narrative, offers an entirely different position from which to view and evaluate the developmental process. And Tisdell, in her chapter on spiritual development, suggests that the ultimate meaning adults give to their lives provides yet another way to understand the developmental process. The richness and variety of these approaches impresses us greatly, and we suspect that this approach to adult development will continue to expand and to exert a growing influence on our understanding of the life course.

Implications for Adult Learning

As we noted at the outset of this chapter, the literature on adult development has had a far-reaching impact on the field of adult education, particularly in shaping the theory and practice of adult learning. In the past those linkages have related primarily to how we can teach most effectively. We have been sensitive to how the biological changes of aging affect learning, for example, or how various life events create incentives for adults to participate in adult education experiences. These insights and others like them are all valuable, and they will continue to shape our practice. But this newer literature on adult development seems to be influencing our field in another way.

We are now being challenged to interpret our professional experience in new ways. In a real sense we are prodded to see what used to be less visible and to hear what was formerly unspoken. We can no longer ignore or take for granted issues of "otherness": gender, race and ethnicity, class, sexual orientation, religious commitment, social status. . . . The list has no end. We must take difference seriously. It is being taken very seriously in the literature on adult development, and it must be taken seriously in adult education as well. This, of course, is already happening, but the point cannot be overemphasized. Awareness of the changes in the adult developmental literature is just one more reminder of this.

We're also being invited to think more creatively about the impact of development on our students. New metaphors provide new insights, and these can only benefit our field. We believe that we will continue to refine our practice as we learn more about development; there is no reason to believe this trend will change. But we suspect that more attention will be given to the interaction of learning and development in the future, especially to the impact of one on the other. However it plays out, we are certain that the connection between adult development and adult learning will continue to be a fruitful one.

References

Caffarella, R. S., and Olson, S. K. "Psychosocial Development of Women: A Critical Review of the Literature." *Adult Education Quarterly,* 1994, 43 (3), 125–151.

Erikson, E. H. *The Lifecycle Completed: A Review.* New York: Norton, 1982.

Gilligan, C. *In a Different Voice: Psychological Theory and Women's Development.* Cambridge, Mass.: Harvard University Press, 1982.

Knowles, M. S. *Modern Practice of Adult Education: From Pedagogy to Andragogy.* (2nd ed.) New York: Association Press, 1980.

Kohlberg, L. "Continuities in Childhood and Adult Moral Development." In P. Baltes and K. Schaie (eds.), *Life-Span Developmental Psychology: Personality and Socialization.* Orlando, Fla.: Academic Press, 1973.

Levinson, D. J. "A Conception of Adult Development." *American Psychologist,* 1986, 41 (1), 3–13.

Maslow, A. H. *Motivation and Personality.* (2nd ed.) New York: HarperCollins, 1970.

Merriam, S. B., and Caffarella, R. S. *Learning in Adulthood: A Comprehensive Guide.* San Francisco: Jossey-Bass, 1999.

ROSEMARY S. CAFFARELLA *is professor of educational leadership at the University of Northern Colorado, Greeley.*

M. CAROLYN CLARK *is associate professor of adult education at Texas A&M University, College Station.*

INDEX

"Absolute knowing" stage, 32
Achievement value, 33
Adult development, 1–2; biological perspectives on, 1, 5, 9–16; defining, 3–4; gender and, 1, 6, 29–36; learning and, 97–100; narrative perspective on, 77–85; psychological perspectives on, 1, 5–6, 19–26; race and ethnicity and, 39–46; separation-connection balance in, 59–66; sexual identity and, 49–56; spiritual dimension of, 2, 5, 87–95; time influences on, 67–74
Adult development field, 3
Adult development theories, 3–7; biological, 1, 5, 9–16; gender bias in, 24, 60–61, 90; gender-related, 29–36; integrating separation and connection, 59–66; narrative, 77–85; psychological, 1, 5–6, 19–26; race- and ethnicity-related, 39–46; of sexual identity and orientation, 49–56; spiritual dimensions and, 87–95; time as integrative dimension in, 67–74; typology of, 1, 4–7, 98–99
Adult learning and education, 1–2; adult development and, 97–100; biological models of adult development and, 16; developmental outcomes or intentions of, 65–66; gender-related models and, 35–36; narrative approach and, 82–84; psychological models of adult development and, 25–26; race/ethnicity and, 44–46; separation-connection and, 63–66; sexual orientation and, 55–56; spiritual development and, 89, 93–94; time dimensions and, 73–74
Adulthood: defining, 4
African Americans: life expectancy of, 10; spirituality and community connection of, 88, 92–93, 94
African Americans' development: of racial identity, 41–42; women's versus men's, 34
Afro-Surinamese women, 53
Age: of adulthood, 4; concepts of, 10; in stage/phase theories, 22, 23. See also Chronological age
Age-graded influences, 6, 68–69
Age ideology, 13, 16
Age-irrelevant society, 69
Ageism, 13
Ageless Body, Timeless Mind (Chopra), 14–15, 15
Aging, 1, 5, 9–16, 98; external changes of, 11; historical time and, 68; internal changes of, 11; mind-body connection in, 10, 12–16; Native American perspectives on, 43; primary and secondary, 10–11, 16; psychological age and, 10; theories of, 11–13. See also Biological development
Ahmed, R., 72, 74
AIDS epidemic, 71, 72
Alternative medicine, 15–16
Alzheimer's disease, 11
American Psychiatric Association, 50–51
Anatomy of an Illness (Cousins), 15
Ancient Greek physicians, 14
Anderson, D. Y., 33, 35–36, 36
Anderson, N. B., 13, 16
Andragogy, 73, 97
Androcentrism, 30–31

Antioxidants, 12
Anzaldua, G., 91, 94
Asian American women, 91
Atherosclerosis, 12
Autonomy, 98; adult education supportive of, 36, 97; white American value of, 43, 89, 90. See also Separation

Bailey, J. M., 51, 56
Baltes, P. B., 6, 7, 67–70, 74
Bateson, C. M., 53, 56
Baumgartner, L. M., 71, 74
Baxter Magolda, M. B., 36
Bee, H. L., 4, 5, 7, 10–11, 16, 20, 26, 60, 66
Being-in-time, 82
Belenky, M., 24, 26
Bem, S. L., 30–31, 36
Bergman, S. J., 60, 61–62, 66
Bielby, D. D., 6, 7
Biller, H. B., 31, 36
Biofeedback, 15, 16
Biological clock, 11–12
Biological definition of race, 40
Biological development, 1, 5, 9–16; age-graded influences and, 6, 68–69, 71–72; anxiety about, 9; concepts and processes of, 9–11; implications of, for adult learning, 16; mind-body connection and, 10–16, 12–13; new perspectives on, 13–16; theories of aging and, 11–13. See also Aging
Biological research on sexual identity development, 51
Bisexuality, 52–53, 55. See also Sexual identity and orientation development
Black Christian churches, 92
Blood glucose levels, 12
Boundary problems, 64
Bridges, W., 23–24, 26
Britzman, D. P., 55–56, 56
Brooks, A. K., 1, 51, 54–55, 56, 57, 99
Brown, L. S., 51, 52, 56
Bruner, J., 78, 83, 85
Bullough, B., 53, 56
Bullough, V., 53, 56
Burg, M. A., 16
Burr, V., 30, 31, 36
Butler, J. P., 54, 56

Caffarella, R. S., 1, 2, 3, 5, 6, 7, 8, 11, 17, 20, 27, 33, 36, 73, 74, 91, 95, 97, 98, 100
Caloric restriction, 12
Cardiovascular disease, 11
Caring, ethic of, 32, 61
Cass, V. C., 51–52, 56
Castillo, A., 91, 94
Catholicism, 91
Caucasians: life expectancy of, 10
Change, narrative as mediator of, 83, 84. See also Transformational learning
Chávez, A. F., 1, 39, 40, 44, 46, 47, 99

Back Issue/Subscription Order Form

Copy or detach and send to:
Jossey-Bass, A Wiley Company, 989 Market Street, San Francisco CA 94103-1741

Call or fax tollfree: **Phone 888-378-2537 6AM-5PM PST; Fax 800-605-2665**

Back issues: Please send me the following issues at $27 each
(Important: please include series initials and issue number, such as ACE90)

1. ACE _____

_____

$ _____Total for single issues

$ _____ SHIPPING CHARGES: SURFACE   Domestic   Canadian

		First Item	$5.00	$6.50
First Item	$5.00	$6.50
Each Add'l Item	$3.00	$3.00

For next-day and second-day delivery rates, call the number listed above.

Subscriptions: Please ❑ start ❑ renew my subscription to *New Directions for Adult and Continuing Education* for the year 2____ at the following rate:

U.S.	❑ Individual $65	❑ Institutional $135
Canada	❑ Individual $65	❑ Institutional $175
All Others	❑ Individual $89	❑ Institutional $209

$ _____Total single issues and subscriptions (Add appropriate sales tax for your state for single issue orders. No sales tax for U.S. subscriptions. Canadian residents, add GST for subscriptions and single issues.)

Federal Tax ID 135593032   GST 89102 8052

❑ Payment enclosed (U.S. check or money order only)

❑ VISA, MC, AmEx, Discover Card # _____ Exp. date_____

Signature _____ Day phone _____

❑ Bill me (U.S. institutional orders only. Purchase order required)

Purchase order #_____

Name _____

Address _____

_____

Phone_____ E-mail _____

For more information about Jossey-Bass, visit our Web site at: www.josseybass.com

PROMOTION CODE = ND3

United States Postal Service

Statement of Ownership, Management, and Circulation

1. Publication Title	2. Publication Number	3. Filing Date
NEW DIRECTIONS FOR ADULT AND CONTINUING EDUCATION	0 1 9 5 – 2 2 4 2	9/30/99

4. Issue Frequency	5. Number of Issues Published Annually	6. Annual Subscription Price
QUARTERLY	4	$56 – indiv. $99 – instit.

7. Complete Mailing Address of Known Office of Publication *(Not printer)* *(Street, city, county, state, and ZIP+4)*	Contact Person
350 SANSOME STREET SAN FRANCISCO, CA 94104 (SAN FRANCISCO COUNTY)	ROGER HUNT
	Telephone (415) 782-3232

8. Complete Mailing Address of Headquarters or General Business Office of Publisher *(Not printer)*

SAME AS ABOVE

9. Full Names and Complete Mailing Addresses of Publisher, Editor, and Managing Editor *(Do not leave blank)*

Publisher *(Name and complete mailing address)*

JOSSEY-BASS INC., PUBLISHERS
(ABOVE ADDRESS)

Editor *(Name and complete mailing address)* SUSAN IMEL, CTR FOR TRAINING & EMPLOYMENT
OHIO STATE UNIVERSITY
1900 KENNY ROAD
COLUMBUS, OH 43210-1090

Managing Editor *(Name and complete mailing address)*

NONE

10. Owner *(Do not leave blank. If the publication is owned by a corporation, give the name and address of the corporation immediately followed by the names and addresses of all stockholders owning or holding 1 percent or more of the total amount of stock. If not owned by a corporation, give the names and addresses of the individual owners. If owned by a partnership or other unincorporated firm, give its name and address as well as those of each individual owner. If the publication is published by a nonprofit organization, give its name and address.)*

Full Name	Complete Mailing Address
JOHN WILEY & SONS INC.	605 THIRD AVENUE NEW YORK, NY 10158-0012

11. Known Bondholders, Mortgagees, and Other Security Holders Owning or Holding 1 Percent or More of Total Amount of Bonds, Mortgages, or Other Securities. If none, check box ———▶ ☐ None

Full Name	Complete Mailing Address
SAME AS ABOVE	SAME AS ABOVE

12. Tax Status *(For completion by nonprofit organizations authorized to mail at nonprofit rates) (Check one)*
The purpose, function, and nonprofit status of this organization and the exempt status for federal income tax purposes:
☐ Has Not Changed During Preceding 12 Months
☐ Has Changed During Preceding 12 Months *(Publisher must submit explanation of change with this statement)*

PS Form **3526**, September 1998   *(See Instructions on Reverse)*

---

13. Publication Title	14. Issue Date for Circulation Data Below
NEW DIRECTIONS FOR ADULT AND CONTINUING EDUCATION	SPRING 1999

15.	Extent and Nature of Circulation	Average No. Copies Each Issue During Preceding 12 Months	No. Copies of Single Issue Published Nearest to Filing Date
a. Total Number of Copies *(Net press run)*		1636	1629
b. Paid and/or Requested Circulation	(1) Paid/Requested Outside-County Mail Subscriptions Stated on Form 3541. *(Include advertiser's proof and exchange copies)*	717	687
	(2) Paid In-County Subscriptions *(Include advertiser's proof and exchange copies)*	0	0
	(3) Sales Through Dealers and Carriers, Street Vendors, Counter Sales, and Other Non-USPS Paid Distribution	0	0
	(4) Other Classes Mailed Through the USPS	0	0
c. Total Paid and/or Requested Circulation *(Sum of 15b. (1), (2),(3),and (4))* ▶		717	687
d. Free Distribution by Mail *(Samples, compliment ary, and other free)*	(1) Outside-County as Stated on Form 3541		
	(2) In-County as Stated on Form 3541		
	(3) Other Classes Mailed Through the USPS	141	175
e. Free Distribution Outside the Mail *(Carriers or other means)*		55	55
f. Total Free Distribution *(Sum of 15d. and 15e.)* ▶		196	230
g. Total Distribution *(Sum of 15c. and 15f)* ▶		913	917
h. Copies not Distributed		723	712
i. Total *(Sum of 15g. and h.)* ▶		1636	1629
j. Percent Paid and/or Requested Circulation *(15c. divided by 15g. times 100)*		78%	75%

16. Publication of Statement of Ownership
☒ Publication required. Will be printed in the WINTER 1999 issue of this publication.   ☐ Publication not required.

17. Signature and Title of Editor, Publisher, Business Manager, or Owner	Date
Susan E. Lewis SUSAN E LEWIS PERIODICALS DIRECTOR	9/30/99

I certify that all information furnished on this form is true and complete. I understand that anyone who furnishes false or misleading information on this form or who omits material or information requested on the form may be subject to criminal sanctions (including fines and imprisonment) and/or civil sanctions (including civil penalties).

Instructions to Publishers

1. Complete and file one copy of this form with your postmaster annually on or before October 1. Keep a copy of the completed form for your records.

2. In cases where the stockholder or security holder is a trustee, include in items 10 and 11 the name of the person or corporation for whom the trustee is acting. Also include the names and addresses of individuals who are stockholders who own or hold 1 percent or more of the total amount of bonds, mortgages, or other securities of the publishing corporation. In item 11, if none, check the box. Use blank sheets if more space is required.

3. Be sure to furnish all circulation information called for in item 15. Free circulation must be shown in items 15d, e, and f.

4. Item 15h., Copies not Distributed, must include (1) newsstand copies originally stated on Form 3541, and returned to the publisher, (2) estimated returns from news agents, and (3), copies for office use, leftovers, spoiled, and all other copies not distributed.

5. If the publication had Periodicals authorization as a general or requester publication, this Statement of Ownership, Management, and Circulation must be published; it must be printed in any issue in October or, if the publication is not published during October, the first issue printed after October.

6. In item 16, indicate the date of the issue in which this Statement of Ownership will be published.

7. Item 17 must be signed.

Failure to file or publish a statement of ownership may lead to suspension of Periodicals authorization.

PS Form **3526**, September 1998 *(Reverse)*

5632 041

→ Adolescent sexuality — how do the
learn?
→ media — scripting
→

WITHDRAWAL